About the Fraser Institute

The **Fraser Institute** is an independer[t] and educational organization. It has attention to the role of competitive m[arkets for] Canadians. Where markets work, the In[stitute's] interest lies in trying to discover prospects for improvement. Where markets do not work, its interest lies in finding the reasons. Where competitive markets have been replaced by government control, the interest of the Institute lies in documenting objectively the nature of the improvement or deterioration resulting from government intervention.

The **Fraser Institute** is a national, federally-chartered, non-profit organization financed by the sale of its publications and the tax-deductible contributions of its members, foundations, and other supporters; it receives no government funding.

Ordering publications

To order additional copies of this book, any of our other publications, or a catalogue of the Institute's publications, please contact the book-sales coordinator: via our **toll-free order line: 1.800.665.3558, ext. 580;** via telephone: 604.688.0221, ext. 580; via fax: 604.688.8539; via e-mail: sales@fraserinstitute.ca.

Media

For media information, please contact Suzanne Walters, Director of Communications: via telephone: 604.714.4582; via e-mail: suzannew@fraserinstitute.ca

Website

To learn more about the Institute and to read our publications on line,
please visit our web site at www.fraserinstitute.ca.

Membership

For information about membership in The Fraser Institute, please contact the Development Department: The Fraser Institute, 4th Floor, 1770 Burrard Street, Vancouver, BC, V6J 3G7; or via telephone: 604.688.0221 ext. 586; via fax: 604.688.8539; via e-mail: membership@fraserinstitute.ca.

In **Calgary**, please contact us via telephone: 403.216.7175;
via fax 403.234.9010;
via e-mail: barrym@fraserinstitute.ca.

In **Toronto**, please contact us via telephone: 416.363.6575;
via fax: 416.934.1639.

Publication

Editing and design by Lindsey Thomas Martin & Kristin McCahon
Cover design by Brian Creswick @ GoggleBox.

Tax Facts 13

Tax Facts 13

by Niels Veldhuis, Joel Emes,
and Michael Walker

The Fraser Institute
Vancouver   Calgary   Toronto
2003

National Library of Canada Cataloguing in Publication Data

Veldhuis, Niels, 1977-
    Tax facts 13 / by Niels Veldhuis, Joel Emes, and Michael Walker.

    Includes bibliographical references.
    ISBN 0-88975-203-6

    1. Taxation--Canada.   2. Tax incidence--Canada.   I. Walker, Michael, 1945-
II. Emes, Joel, 1968-   III. Fraser Institute (Vancouver, B.C.)   IV. Title.   V. Title:
Tax facts thirteen.

HJ2449.V44 2003   336.2´00971   C2003-910750-7

Contents

Tables and Figures

Tables

Figures

About the Authors

JOEL EMES is a Senior Analyst with the BC Progress Board. From 1996 to 2002, he was senior research economist at The Fraser Institute, where he was the primary researcher for Tax Freedom Day and the Institute's provincial and state-provincial fiscal comparisons, the Budget Performance Index and the Fiscal Performance Index. He was also a regular contributor to the Fraser Institute's monthly magazine, *Fraser Forum*. He was co-author of *Tax Facts 10, 11,* and *12* and of *Canadian Government Debt* (1996, 1998, 1999, and 2003 editions). His articles have appeared in the *National Post*, the *Globe and Mail*, the *Calgary Herald*, the *Vancouver Sun* and the *London Free Press*. He received his M.A. in Economics from Simon Fraser University in 1995.

NIELS VELDHUIS is Senior Research Economist at The Fraser Institute. He holds a Bachelors degree in Business Administration, with joint majors in business and economics and a Masters Degree in Economics from Simon Fraser University. His recent publications and co-publications for The Fraser Institute include *Canadian Government Debt 2003: A Guide to the Indebtedness of Canada and the Provinces* (2003), *Ontario Prosperity: Is Best of Second Best Good Enough?* (2003), *Measuring Labour Markets in Canada and the United States* (2003), and *Tax and Expenditure Limitations: The Next Step in Fiscal Discipline* (2003). Mr Veldhuis is also the primary researcher for Tax Freedom Day. He writes *Questions & Answers* in *Fraser Forum*, the Fraser Institute's monthly magazine. His articles have appeared in various newspapers across the country, including such dailies as *The Province, The Vancouver Sun, The Victoria Times-Colonist, The Calgary Sun, The Calgary Herald, The Winnipeg Free Press, The Saskatoon StarPhoenix, The Ottawa Citizen, The National Post,* and *The Toronto Star.* He has appeared as a commentator on various television programs including *BCTV News* and the *Global National News.*

MICHAEL WALKER is an economist, journalist, broadcaster, consultant, university lecturer and public speaker. As an economist, he has written or edited 50 books on economic topics. His articles on technical economic subjects have appeared in professional journals in Canada, the United States and Europe, including the *Canadian Journal of Economics*, the

American Economic Review, The *Journal of Finance,* the *Canadian Tax Journal, Health Management Quarterly* and *Health Affairs.*

As a journalist, he has written some 700 articles which have appeared in some 60 newspapers, including *The Globe and Mail,* the *Wall Street Journal, The Vancouver Sun, The Chicago Tribune, Reader's Digest,* the *Detroit News,* and the *Western Star*—the latter being the newspaper in his birthplace, Corner Brook, Newfoundland. He has been a regular columnist in *The Vancouver Province, The Toronto Sun,* and the *Ottawa Citizen.*

As a broadcaster, he has written and delivered some 2,000 radio broadcasts on economic topics and appeared on radio and television programs in Canada, the United States, and Latin America. As a consultant, he has provided advice to private groups and governments in the United States, Argentina, Australia, Bermuda, Brazil, Chile, Germany, Hong Kong, Jamaica, New Zealand, Mexico, Panama, Peru, Sweden, Venezuela and Canada. He has lectured to over 2000 audiences at universities and in other venues on five continents.

Since 1974, Michael Walker has directed the activities of The Fraser Institute. Before that, he taught at the University of Western Ontario and Carleton University and was employed at the Bank of Canada and the Federal Department of Finance. He received his Ph.D. at the University of Western Ontario and his B.A. at St. Francis Xavier University.

He is a director of a number of firms and other enterprises, including Mancal Corporation and The Milton and Rose D. Friedman Foundation. He is on the *Financial Post* Board of Economists. In 1992, he was awarded the Colin M. Brown Freedom Medal and Award by the National Citizens' Coalition and, in 2003, he received an honorary Doctor of Laws degree (LL.D) from The University of Western Ontario. He is married and has two children.

Acknowledgments

We are pleased to acknowledge the assistance of Statistics Canada, which provided certain unpublished background data essential to this study. The Canadian Tax Simulator computer programs were originally written by David Gill whose unsparing efforts we are pleased to acknowledge.

The sixth and seventh editions of *Tax Facts* were computed on a set of programs modified to run on a microcomputer system. These modifications were completed by Douglas T. Wills. The eighth, ninth, and tenth editions were computed using the SPSS statistical package with programming provided by Filip Palda and Isabella Horry. The eleventh and twelfth editions were computed using Statistics Canada's Social Policy Simulation Database and Model (SPSD/M) and the SPSS statistical package. SPSD/M programming was provided by Joel Emes and SPSS programming was provided by Joel Emes using the framework established by Filip Palda and Isabella Horry.

The authors would like to express their gratitude to all those involved in the production and release of this book. The authors, of course, take full and complete responsibility for any remaining errors or omissions.

Disclaimer

A portion of this analysis is based on Statistics Canada's Social Policy Simulation Database and Model (SPSD/M). The assumptions and calculations underlying the simulation results were prepared by the authors and the responsibility for the use and interpretation of these data is entirely theirs.

Preface

THIS BOOK IS A SUMMARY OF THE LATEST RESULTS of a Fraser Institute project that began in July, 1975. Its objective was to find out how much tax, in all forms, Canadians pay to federal, provincial, and municipal governments and how the size of this tax bill has changed over the years since 1961. In the interim, 12 editions of this book have been published.

The book has been written with two distinct purposes in mind: first, to provide a non-technical do-it-yourself manual so that the average Canadian family can estimate how much tax it pays; and second, to update a statistic, first published in 1976, that we call the Canadian Consumer Tax Index. This index measures how much the tax bill of an average Canadian family has increased since 1961 and by how much it is changing currently. In other words, it measures changes in the price that Canadians pay for government.

This book does not attempt to look at the benefits that Canadians receive from government in return for their taxes. Rather, it looks at the price that is paid for a product—government. It has nothing to say about the quality of the product, how much of it each of us receives, or whether we get our money's worth. These questions are, however, considered in various publications of the Fraser Institute, including *Government Spending Facts 2*, and our government report cards.

Many of the recent statistics contained in this book are based on output from Statistics Canada's Social Policy Simulation Database and Model (SPSD/M), a microsimulation model of the Canadian tax and transfer system. Prior to 1992, the analysis was done with group average data pre-compiled by Statistics Canada. Because the analysis is now built up from families, it is possible to examine the situation of particular types of taxpayers with a good deal more precision.

The Fraser Institute's calculations of the tax burden are part of an on-going program of research. In making these results available to the public we seek both to inform and to be informed. Readers who disagree with our methods or conclusions are invited to write to the Institute to convey the nature of their reservations. In this way, our methods and our estimates can be refined and perfected.

—Michael A. Walker

Tax Facts 13

Chapter 1
The Canadian Tax System

Undoubtedly, one of the most unpopular policies in Canadian history was the introduction of the Goods and Services Tax (GST) in 1991. In part, its political unpopularity was due to the fact that many Canadians thought that this was a new tax that would increase the tax burden. But, it also reflected a deep-seated concern on the part of citizens about the process of government and revealed the belief held by many that the government was collecting too many tax dollars while accomplishing too little in the way of public services.

The most significant revelation in the reaction to the GST, however, was that the Canadian public has very little real information about the tax system. Very few knew that the GST was replacing a tax already in place and fewer still realized that the federal government's main ambition was not to raise more revenue but rather to replace the Manufacturers' Tax. Everyone who had studied the Manufacturers' Tax had concluded that it was a terrible tax that had many unintended negative effects. It was a tax that needed to be replaced but Canadians' ignorance about it was a significant barrier to its removal. While some would say that there is no such thing as a good tax, it is the case that, as long as there is a demand for public expenditures, there will have to be taxes to finance them. We now know that taxes distort people's decisions, leaving opportunities for mutually beneficial exchanges unexploited. The task, then, is to design an efficient set of taxes, one that does not unduly interfere with the types of decisions people make in the marketplace.

There is, then, something worse than a tax and that is a badly de-signed tax, which, in addition to taking spending power from the private sector, also distorts everyday decisions in a way that is neither desirable nor necessary. As free international trade becomes a reality, it is increas-ingly important that governments implement efficient and sensibly de-signed tax systems. A prerequisite to being able to debate and design such taxes is a base of information about them. The purpose of this book is to provide a basic tool kit of knowledge about taxation in Canada in order to enhance the opportunity for rational debate about these issues.

This book is an important resource for everyone concerned about the extent and relatively rapid growth of taxation in this country. Between 1981 and 2003, the total tax bill of the average Canadian family from all three levels of government increased in real terms by $7,412 in 2003 dol-lars. Figure 1.1 charts the progress of taxes for selected years since 1981.

The many faces of the tax collector

The Canadian tax system is continually changing. To understand current developments it is important to know how the Canadian taxation system

---

Figure 1.1: Federal, provincial, and municipal taxes collected from the average Canadian family, 1981–2003 ($2003)

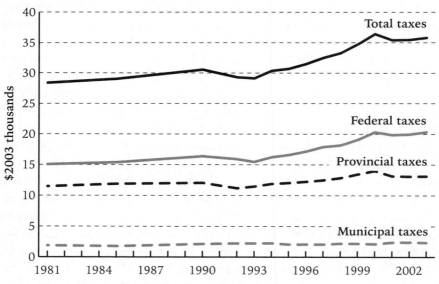

Source: The Fraser Institute's Canadian Tax Simulator 2003.

has evolved. Under the Canadian Constitution, the federal and provincial governments are essentially given unlimited powers of taxation. Under the British North America Act, the immediate predecessor of the Canadian Constitution, the federal parliament has the power to raise money by any mode or system of taxation while the provinces are limited to collecting taxes that are paid directly by the person being taxed—so-called direct taxes. But, because of the broad judicial interpretation of the meaning of the word "direct," the provinces have been able to levy all sorts of taxes, except for import duties and taxes on sales that cross provincial borders. Given this unlimited scope for taxation and more than 125 years of ingenuity, it is not surprising that Canada now has a very complicated tax system. See Lewis (1978), J. Harvey Perry (1989) and David B. Perry (1997) for further information on the Canadian tax system's evolution.

Figure 1.2 shows the 34 revenue categories used in the determination of Equalization[1] payments. Considering that many of these revenue sources are affected by multiple rates, depreciation allowances, tax credits, and surcharges gives some indication of the complexity of Canada's tax system.

Income taxes predominate

Table 1.1 and figure 1.3 show that personal income taxes are the largest single source of government revenue. During 2002, some $141 billion was extracted by federal and provincial income tax—37.0% of the total taxes that Canadians pay. Second as a source of federal and provincial revenues was sales tax—16.0% of tax revenue and $61 billion in taxes. Taxes on corporate profits—9.1% of total taxes—accounted for a further $34 billion, while taxes on property and natural resources accounted for $56 billion, or 14.6%. Together, these five kinds of tax accounted for 76.7% of total government revenue during 2002. Just under one-half of government tax revenue comes from personal income tax and the tax on corporate profits, which were implemented in 1916 and 1917 as "temporary" measures to finance World War I.

Table 1.1 also illustrates how the Canadian tax structure has evolved over the 41 years between 1961 and 2002. The most obvious change has been the increased reliance on the personal income tax. While always a

---

1 For a thorough analysis of Canada's equalization system, see Usher 1995. For a brief overview of the determination of equalization payments, see Emes 2002.

Figure 1.2: Revenue sources used in determining equalization payments

1   personal income taxes

2   business income revenues

3   capital tax revenues

4   general and miscellaneous sales taxes

5   tobacco taxes

6   gasoline taxes

7   diesel fuel taxes

8   non-commercial vehicle licenses

9   commercial vehicle licenses

10   revenue from the sale of alcoholic beverages

11   hospital and medical insurance premiums

12   race track taxes

13   forestry revenues

14   new oil revenues less rebates and credits

15   old oil revenues less rebates and credits

16   heavy oil revenues less rebates, credits and oil export charge

17   mined oil revenues less rebates and credits

18   domestically sold natural gas revenues

19   exported natural gas revenues

20   sales of Crown leases less rebates and credits

21   other oil and gas revenues less rebates and credits

22   mineral resources—asbestos

23   mineral resources—coal

24   mineral resources—other

25   potash revenues

26   water power rentals

27   insurance premium taxes

28   payroll taxes

29   provincial and local property taxes less regular property tax credits and related tax credits

30   lottery ticket revenues

31   miscellaneous provincial and local taxes and revenues from the sale of goods and services, including local water revenues

32   shared revenues: offshore activities/Newfoundland

33   shared revenues: offshore activities/Nova Scotia

34   shared revenues: preferred share dividend

Source: Canadian Tax Foundation, *Finances of the Nation 2002*, table 8.4.

Table 1.1: Taxes paid and percent of total taxes, 1961 and 2002

	1961		2002	
	$ millions	percent	$ millions	percent
Personal income taxes	2,099	22.7	140,534	37.0
General sales taxes	1,351	14.6	60,884	16.0
Health & social insurance levies	663	7.2	41,221	10.9
Property & related taxes	1,435	15.5	43,291	11.4
Corporate income taxes	1,199	13.0	34,387	9.1
Liquor, tobacco, & amusement taxes	837	9.1	18,505	4.9
Motive fuel taxes	525	5.7	12,411	3.3
Miscellaneous taxes	55	0.6	3,879	1.0
Natural resource taxes & royalties	266	2.9	12,304	3.2
Privileges, licences & permits	190	2.1	2,919	0.8
Customs duties	438	4.7	3,203	0.8
Other consumption taxes	173	1.9	1,842	0.5
Non-resident taxes	0	0.0	4,360	1.1
Total	9,231		379,740	

Sources: Statistics Canada, Public Institutions Division, cats. 68-211, 68-204, 68-207, 68-213; calculations by the authors.

prominent feature of the tax system, the income tax has in recent years become even more important. In 1961, income taxes represented only 22.7¢ out of every tax dollar Canadians paid but by 2002 income taxes accounted for 37.0¢—almost two-and-one-half times the revenue generated by the next largest source, sales taxes.

This increase came about largely through passive interaction between the progressive income tax system and money incomes swollen by inflation. This interaction is often referred to as "bracket creep" because taxpayers can be pushed into higher tax brackets when their income goes up to compensate them for an increase in the general price level. Until the income tax system was indexed to the inflation rate in 1974, all income increases were taxed at progressively higher rates in spite of the fact that much of the increased income represented illusory inflation-based gains. From 1974 to 1985, brackets and exemptions were increased by an "indexing factor" based on the consumer price index. From 1986 through 2000, the income-tax system was only partially indexed because the indexing factor was set at the amount by which the inflation rate exceeded 3.0%. Partial indexing meant that, although the inflation rate was 5.6%

Figure 1.3a: Where government obtained its revenue, 1961

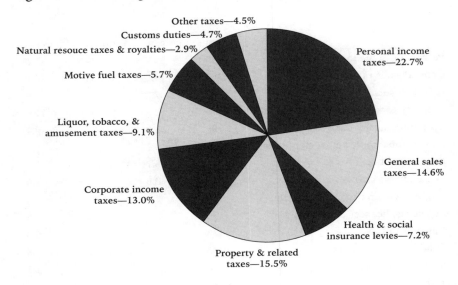

Other taxes—4.5%
Customs duties—4.7%
Natural resouce taxes & royalties—2.9%
Motive fuel taxes—5.7%
Liquor, tobacco, & amusement taxes—9.1%
Corporate income taxes—13.0%
Property & related taxes—15.5%
Health & social insurance levies—7.2%
General sales taxes—14.6%
Personal income taxes—22.7%

Source: Table 1.1; note that percentages may not total 100% due to rounding.

Figure 1.3b: Where government obtained its revenue, 2002

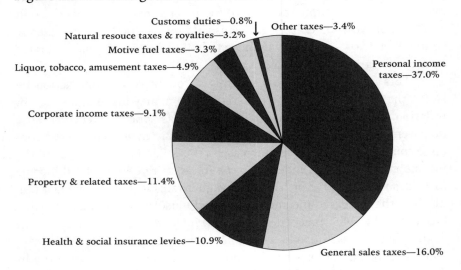

Customs duties—0.8%
Natural resouce taxes & royalties—3.2%
Motive fuel taxes—3.3%
Liquor, tobacco, amusement taxes—4.9%
Other taxes—3.4%
Corporate income taxes—9.1%
Personal income taxes—37.0%
Property & related taxes—11.4%
Health & social insurance levies—10.9%
General sales taxes—16.0%

Source: Table 1.1; note that percentages may not total 100% due to rounding.

in 1991, personal income-tax exemptions and brackets increased by only 2.6% between 1991 and 1992. Exemptions and brackets stayed at their 1992 level until 1998 because inflation has been below 3.0% in every year since 1992. The Organisation for Economic Cooperation and Development (OECD) estimates that between 1988 and 1998, 18% of tax filers were pushed into a higher tax bracket because of partial indexation. In other words, 1.4 million Canadians became taxable because inflation adjustments were made to their incomes but not to their exemptions. Another 1.9 million taxpayers jumped from the 17% to 26% bracket and 0.6 million moved from the 26% to the 29% bracket. The 1998 and 1999 federal budgets increased the amount of money that could be earned before income tax applied and the 2000 federal budget brought back full indexation to the personal income-tax system.

As a consequence of this growth in revenue from personal income taxes, government was able to rely less on other forms of taxation and to allow the burden of some of these taxes to fall. However, in some important cases—notably sales tax and health and social insurance levies—the rate of tax was increased despite rapidly growing revenues from personal income tax. Table 1.2 presents the share of GDP that the top nine taxes represent.

Table 1.2: Total taxes as a percentage of gross domestic product, 1961 and 2002

	1961	2002
Personal income taxes	5.1	12.3
General sales taxes	3.3	5.3
Health & social insurance levies	1.6	3.6
Property & related taxes	3.5	3.8
Corporate income taxes	2.9	3.0
Liquor, tobacco, & amusement taxes	2.0	1.6
Customs duties	1.1	0.3
Motive fuel taxes	1.3	1.1
Natural resources & other taxes	1.7	2.2
Total	22.5	33.2

Sources: Statistics Canada, *Canadian Economic Observer*, cat. 11-010 and Public Institutions Division, cats. 68-211, 68-204, 68-207, 68-213; calculations by the authors.

Sales taxes

While revenue from income tax poured into the federal government's coffers, the provinces were prompted by their desire for additional tax revenue to boost their sales-tax rates. Two general exceptions are Alberta, which has no sales tax, and British Columbia, where the sales tax has been adjusted up and down.

In British Columbia, sales tax was reduced from 7% to 5% on April 11, 1978 and was further reduced to 4% on April 1, 1979. On March 10, 1981, however, it was raised to 6% and, in July 1983, raised again to 7%. In the 1987 budget, the tax was once again dropped to 6% but, in the 1993 budget, raised once more to 7%. Finally, the 2002 budget raised the sales tax rate to 7.5%.

The federal government also sought to increase its revenue from indirect sources in the early and mid-1980s by increasing its takings from the Manufacturers' Sales Tax and, in 1991, by replacing this tax with the more comprehensive GST. The Department of Finance hoped to raise an extra $10 billion annually from this new source.

Taxes on natural resources

The rise in resource taxation in the 1970s and 1980s resulted primarily from increases in the price of oil and gas, triggered by the oil embargo and subsequent cartelization of oil pricing by the OPEC countries in 1973. In the normal course of events, these increases in price in Canada would automatically have meant a sharp rise in the return to Canadian producers. But, the provincial governments absorbed much of this so-called "windfall" or "rent" in the form of higher taxes or royalties. The federal government, for its part, imposed a further tax on producers who were exporting oil. This tax, the oil export charge, amounted to the difference between the controlled Canadian price per barrel and the world price. Proceeds from the federal tax were then used to subsidize imports of foreign oil into the eastern provinces.

From 1974 to 1984, provincial governments and, especially, the federal government escalated their taxation of natural resources. The National Energy Program and the subsequent Energy Agreement allowed the federal government to earn about $4 billion from petroleum during 1984.

The 1985 federal budget incorporated a number of changes to energy taxes as agreed upon in the Western Accord with the governments of

Saskatchewan, Alberta, and British Columbia. Both the oil export charge and the petroleum compensation charge were eliminated. Other energy taxes, such as the Petroleum and Gas Revenue Tax, were revised, reduced and, in some cases, phased out.[2] These changes, combined with the decline in world oil prices, resulted in a decline in energy-related revenues in both relative and absolute terms. The recent increase in oil and gas prices is responsible for the relative and absolute increase in natural resource tax revenue.

More efficient taxation

The late 1980s and early 1990s saw the federal government trying to make income, corporate, and sales taxes more efficient and less of a burden to Canadians competing in the international marketplace. While corporate and income tax rates fell, many deductions were eliminated in order to expand the tax base. These changes were supposed to diminish the degree to which taxes enter into Canadians' decisions. If this principle seems strange, consider a flat tax. The rate of such a tax is not related to any economic activity in which the individual may engage. Government simply takes a fixed proportion of total income no matter how it is earned. The amount that the government takes may be huge but, since the tax is not related to how much an individual works or spends, it will not directly affect decisions between, for example, spending and saving or working and not working. Moreover, since the taxation rate is the same regardless of income, there is no tax disincentive to discourage an effort to move to higher income levels from any given starting income.

Lowering tax rates, however, did not lead to less tax being collected: in the past 18 years, due to the expanding tax base and, more recently, to bracket creep, federal collections from the average family have risen by $4,953 in 2003 dollars. That the federal government has not collected even more taxes is due to its declining commitment to provincial projects such as welfare, education, and health care. In reaction, the provinces have made up the shortfall not by reducing spending but by increasing taxes. Since 1985, provincial collections from the average family have increased by $1,238 in 2003 dollars.

---

2 For more information on oil pricing and taxation, see Watkins and Walker 1977, Watkins and Walker 1981 and chapter 8 of Perry 1997.

Dividing the spoils

How is total tax revenue divided among different levels of government? Table 1.3 provides a breakdown of major taxes by federal, provincial, and municipal levels of government for the years 1961 and 2002. Total taxes collected now amount to 33.2¢ out of every dollar of GDP, a 47.8% rise since 1961 (see table 1.2).

Table 1.3a: Taxes collected by federal, provincial, and municipal governments ($billions)

	Federal		Provincial		Municipal	
	1961	2002	1961	2002	1961	2002
Personal income taxes	2.0	87.6	0.1	52.9	0.0	0.0
Corporate income taxes	0.2	22.0	1.0	12.4	0.0	0.0
General sales taxes	0.3	31.3	1.0	29.5	0.0	0.1
Property & related taxes	0.0	0.0	0.0	8.7	1.3	34.6
Health & social insurance levies	0.5	22.2	0.2	19.0	0.0	0.0
Natural resource revenues	0.0	0.0	0.3	12.3	0.0	0.0
Customs duties	0.5	3.2	0.0	0.0	0.0	0.0
Other taxes	0.6	14.7	1.1	28.6	0.1	0.6
Total	4.8	181.0	2.9	163.5	1.4	35.2

Table 1.3b: Taxes collected by federal, provincial, and municipal governments (% of total)

	Federal		Provincial		Municipal	
	1961	2002	1961	2002	1961	2002
Personal income taxes	95.2	62.3	4.8	37.7	0.0	0.0
Corporate income taxes	16.7	63.9	83.3	36.1	0.0	0.0
General sales taxes	23.1	51.4	76.9	48.4	0.0	0.1
Property & related taxes	0.0	0.0	0.0	20.1	100.0	79.9
Health & social insurance levies	71.4	53.8	28.6	46.2	0.0	0.0
Natural resource revenues	0.0	0.0	100.0	100.0	0.0	0.0
Customs duties	100.0	100.0	0.0	0.0	0.0	0.0
Other taxes	33.3	33.6	61.1	65.2	5.6	1.3
Total	52.7	47.7	31.9	43.1	15.4	9.3

Sources: Statistics Canada, Public Institutions Division, cats. 68-211, 68-204, 68-207, 68-213; calculations by the authors.

These figures give a somewhat distorted impression about which level of government is doing the taxing because some municipal and provincial government revenue comes from other levels of government. For example, in 1961, 30% of provincial and municipal revenues were derived from other levels of government. Provinces received transfers from the federal government while municipalities received transfers from both levels.

In the case of provincial revenues, the figures for 1961 reflect the tax agreement that was in effect between the federal and provincial governments. Under the agreement, the federal government rented the provinces' rights to tax personal incomes: in effect, the provinces relinquished their right to tax personal incomes in return for cash payments from the federal government, which collected all the taxes. Accordingly, the tax-collection statistics for 1961 do not reflect the division of the revenues produced but only which level of government actually collected them.

For 2002, the collection figures match the revenue as it was divided between federal and provincial governments more closely because revenue-sharing agreements have been gradually modified to eliminate tax-rental arrangements and shared-cost programs. In the years following 1978, the provinces have had, increasingly, to find their own revenues. As a consequence, tax receipts from different levels of government reflect the actual sharing of tax revenues more closely. To a considerable degree, this evolution reflects the changing attitudes of the partners in Canadian confederation: changing tax arrangements may be the first steps towards a more decentralized federation. For the 2002/2003 fiscal year, Alberta received about 9.2% of its revenue from the federal government. This gives Alberta considerably more flexibility when they decide whether or not to participate in new or ongoing federal programs than, for example, Newfoundland, which receives about 39% of its revenue from federal sources. Zelder (2000) shows how Alberta and Ontario could reform their health-care systems and save money, even if the reforms contravened the Canada Health Act and caused the federal government to stop all Canada Health and Social Transfers to the two provinces.

The relationship between provincial and municipal government revenues reflects a different process. Municipalities now collect much less of their total revenue in the form of taxes than they did in 1961: fully 38.8% of municipal revenue is now accounted for by transfers from federal and provincial governments, mainly the latter. In large part, the emerging role of municipalities as dependencies of the provincial governments is a result of decreasing reliance on property taxation as a form of finance (see table 1.1 and figure 1.3). Property taxes accounted for only 11.4% of total taxes in 2002, down from 15.5% in 1961.

The fifth column—hidden taxation

Most people are aware of the prominent direct taxes that they pay— income tax and property tax. Many others correctly regard contributions by employees and employers to the Employment Insurance fund and the Canada and Quebec Pension Plans as taxes. Moreover, many people know how much of these taxes they pay as the information is provided on pay stubs, (e.g. income tax and contributions to EI and CPP/QPP) and annual property-tax assessments. There is, however, another class of taxes of which Canadians, by and large, are unaware. These taxes are built into the price of goods and services and are often not identified to the final consumer as a tax. These are known as "indirect" or "hidden" taxes.

Indirect taxes

The most well known of the indirect taxes are import duties, the excise taxes on items such as tobacco and alcohol, and the federal Goods and Services Tax (GST). GST legislation requires sellers to make it clear to purchasers whether the GST is included in the listed price or if it will be added when the sale is totalled. Although consumers are made aware of the tax because of this requirement, few will have a good idea of the total amount of GST they pay in a year. Other, less familiar, indirect taxes are levied on many common products. The excise taxes on such items as tobacco, alcohol, and gasoline are good examples. See figures 1.4 and 1.5 for a break-down of taxes paid for a litre of gasoline and for a bottle of liquor. Table 1.4 shows the province-by-province break-down of the pump price of gasoline. In the case of liquor, the federal rate of indirect tax is 116%. In addition, alcohol bears the provincial government's mark-up as well as a provincial sales tax. The final delivered price of alcohol is 534% above the price received by the distiller. The taxes on tobacco were so high that they led to widespread smuggling and tax evasion until 1994 when taxes were sharply reduced east of the Manitoba border; the western provinces stepped up enforcement instead of cutting taxes. Smuggling had become so bad that, as Ontario's finance minister at the time put it, "It reached a point where the retail market in cigarettes in Ontario was in complete shambles." (McInnes 1996: A1, A4). However, in 2002 the federal government and every provincial government increased tobacco taxes. Most consumers of these products are aware that gasoline, alcohol, and tobacco are

Figure 1.4: Government take from a litre of gasoline (Canadian average; in cents per litre)

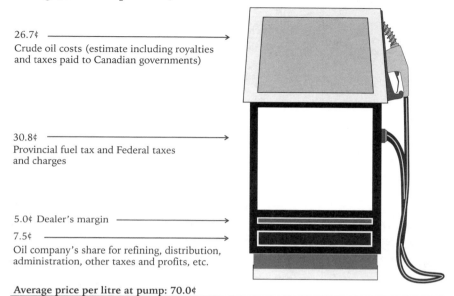

26.7¢ ————————————————→
Crude oil costs (estimate including royalties
and taxes paid to Canadian governments)

30.8¢ ————————————————→
Provincial fuel tax and Federal taxes
and charges

5.0¢ Dealer's margin ————————→

7.5¢ ————————————————→
Oil company's share for refining, distribution,
administration, other taxes and profits, etc.

Average price per litre at pump: 70.0¢

Source: Canadian Petroleum Products Institute, *Fuel Facts 4, 12* (June 24, 2003)
(all editions).

Table 1.4: Components of the price of gasoline (in cents/litre for regular unleaded gasoline at self-serve pumps), by city

	Crude cost (estimate)	Refiner Margin	Marketer Margin	Taxes	Pump Price
Vancouver	28.5	8.8	3.2	35.5	76.0
Edmonton	27.3	9.0	6.6	23.3	66.2
Regina	27.3	9.6	6.3	29.8	73.0
Winnipeg	27.3	10.0	0.3	25.6	63.2
Toronto	27.0	6.1	5.8	29.1	68.0
Montreal	25.2	6.8	4.8	36.3	73.1
Saint John	24.6	7.2	8.0	34.2	74.0
Halifax	24.6	7.2	6.0	35.0	72.8
Charlottetown*	24.6	7.2	8.1	28.5	68.4
St. John's*	24.6	8.4	9.2	36.8	79.0
Canadian Average	26.7	7.5	5.0	30.8	70.0

Source: Canadian Petroleum Products Institute, *Fuel Facts* 4, 12 (June 24, 2003)
(all editions). * regulated markets.

Figure 1.5: Typical government take from a bottle of liquor

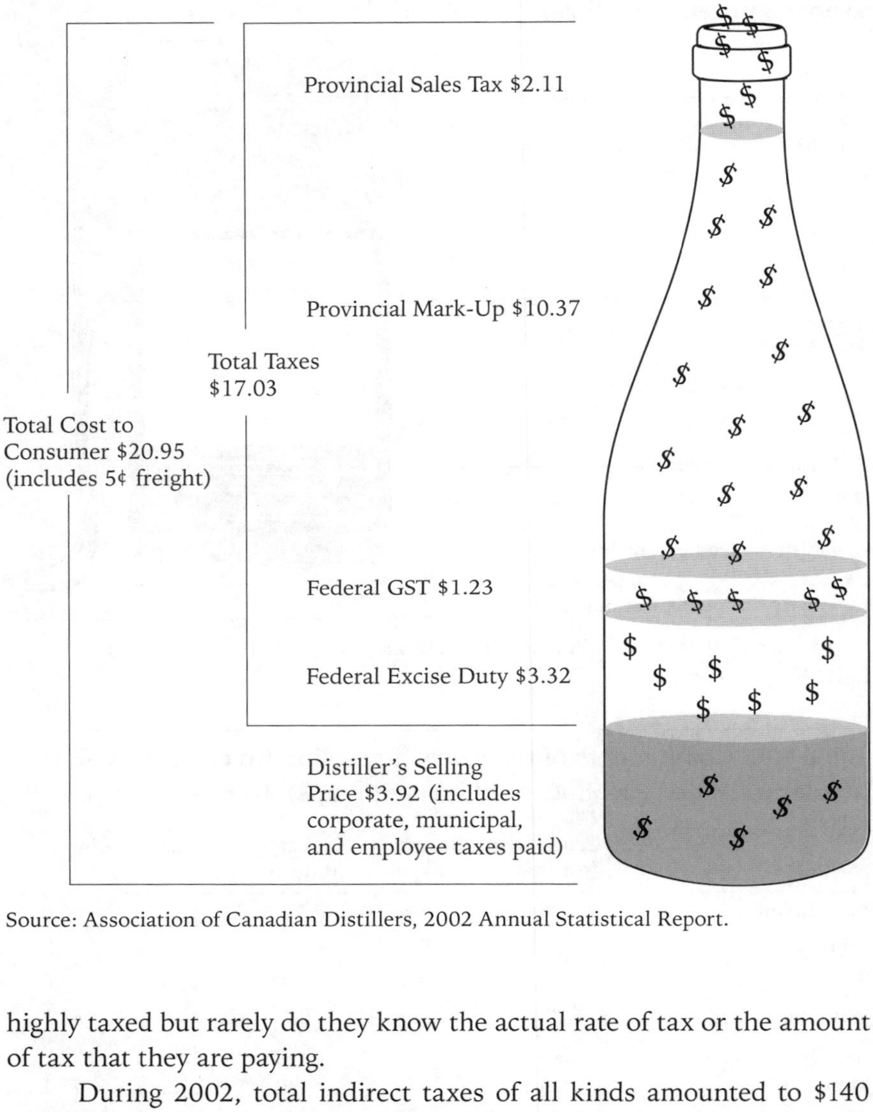

Provincial Sales Tax $2.11

Provincial Mark-Up $10.37

Total Taxes
$17.03

Total Cost to
Consumer $20.95
(includes 5¢ freight)

Federal GST $1.23

Federal Excise Duty $3.32

Distiller's Selling
Price $3.92 (includes
corporate, municipal,
and employee taxes paid)

Source: Association of Canadian Distillers, 2002 Annual Statistical Report.

highly taxed but rarely do they know the actual rate of tax or the amount of tax that they are paying.

During 2002, total indirect taxes of all kinds amounted to $140 billion in Canada. This was 12.3% of total Canadian income and accounted for 36.9% of total government revenue from taxation. In other words, quite apart from the tax they pay when they receive their incomes, Canadians pay, on average, a further 12.3% in indirect taxes when they spend their income. Furthermore, over one-third of all government revenue is collected in this indirect, hidden form.

The hot potatoes—passing tax forward

Hidden taxes are hard to calculate because people try to pass them on to others—any tax that can be avoided is money in one's own pocket. As a result, people throughout the economy are constantly avoiding situations in which they will have to pay taxes and seeking to pay as little tax as possible when they cannot avoid them. The moonlighting tradesperson who engages in "cash only" transactions, the mechanic who fixes his neighbour's truck in return for free cartage, the dentist who fixes the teeth of a fellow dentist's family on a reciprocal basis, the tycoon whose business is incorporated in the Turks and Caicos Islands, all want to avoid taxes. In the end, though, when a tax is levied, somebody ends up paying. One of the most difficult and important questions in economics is to discover who that somebody is; this is known as the study of "tax incidence."

How employees pass the tax on

To get an idea of the difficulties involved, consider the following. The average Canadian employee measures his welfare in terms of after-tax dollars and in each new wage contract bargains for an increase in take-home pay. The fact that an increase in gross terms will imply a smaller increase in after-tax dollars motivates the employee or his union representative to demand a larger gross increase. By doing so, the employee is attempting to get the employer to bear the burden of the additional tax. For an example of this process, see table 1.5.

The employee who bargains in this manner is attempting to pass the tax forward. This behaviour is not unique; it is a general characteristic of all participants in the Canadian economy. Corporations attempt to pass the higher taxes on profits and payroll forward to the consumer in the form of higher prices or backward to employees in the form of lower

---

Table 1.5: Take-home pay versus gross pay

In 2002, a single person in Ontario with an income of $35,000 had to receive a 5.9% raise in pay to realize a 5.0% increase in after-tax pay. Comparable figures for the other provinces are presented below.

NF	PE	NS	NB	QC	ON	MB	SK	AB	BC
6.2%	6.1%	6.2%	6.2%	6.1%	5.9%	6.2%	6.0%	5.9%	5.9%

Source: Sources: Canadian Tax Foundation, Finances of The Nation 2002; calculations by the authors.

wages. The difficulty in measuring the degree to which these attempts are or are not successful greatly complicates the study of tax incidence.

Who pays the indirect taxes?

While it is difficult to know where the burden of these taxes ultimately lies, it is not impossible. We need to make intelligent assumptions about how each tax is passed on. For example, a general sales tax is collected and remitted to government by retailers. It is clear, however, that in most cases the retailers do not actually bear the tax—they are merely the agents for collecting it. The actual effect of the tax is to increase the price of all goods and services affected by the tax and to cause a corresponding reduction in the purchasing power of family incomes. Accordingly, to the extent that a general sales tax causes an increase in the general level of prices, the tax is borne not by the collectors but by income earners in the economy, whose incomes now buy less. Indirect or sales taxes, therefore, burden all income earned in the economy.

Payroll taxes such as Employment Insurance premiums and contributions to the Canada and Quebec Pension Plans are collected, in part, from the employer and, in part, from the employee. And, while no one would dispute that the employee pays the employee's portion, in most cases it is true that the employee also pays the so-called employer's portion. This is because the payroll tax paid by the employer is included in the total amount of money the employer has available to pay labour-related costs. In other words, payroll taxes reduce potential wage and salary payments below what they would otherwise have been. Since no corresponding reduction can be expected in the price of the products that the employee will want to purchase, the payroll tax, in effect, burdens the employee.

While both of these arguments have been framed in terms of employees and their wages and salaries, it is clear that taxes burden capital income as well. For example, a general sales tax reduces the purchasing power of all income, not just wage and salary income. As a result, it is appropriate to view the burden of the general sales tax as falling on all forms of earned income, including interest income and dividends. All of the estimates of tax burden constructed in this study, therefore, allocate the burden of general sales taxes in proportion to all earned income received by a family. In practical terms, this means that if general sales taxes amount to 7% of total Canadian income in a particular year, we add 7% of a family's total earned income to the family's tax bill when we calculate how much tax the family pays.

In computing this burden of general sales tax, income that a family receives from government is explicitly ignored. This is because the payments received from government such as Old Age Security and the Canada Pension Plan have been, and currently are, either directly or indirectly indexed to the general level of prices to offset the effects of inflation. As the general price level rises in step with the sales tax, the purchasing power of transfers from government is not permitted to fall. As a consequence, the general sales tax does not have the effect of burdening income in this form, and it would be inappropriate to allocate any part of the burden of general sales taxes to this sort of income.

While the burdens of a general sales tax and payroll taxes are relatively straightforward to assign, the assignment of particular excise taxes is more elusive. Whereas a general sales tax increases all prices and hence reduces the purchasing power of all incomes not derived from transfers from government, particular taxes on commodities usually affect only the price of that commodity. For example, excise taxes imposed on liquor, motor vehicles, and fuels affect only the prices of those products. Ultimately, of course, they may affect a whole range of prices—fuel taxes and motor vehicle taxes affect the price of transportation. These taxes may, therefore, have an overall effect although levied only on a particular product.

In light of these considerations, it had been the usual practice when calculating tax burdens to allocate the burden of particular excise taxes according to the consumption of those items. Studies of the 1976 tax burden published by The Fraser Institute (Walker 1976; Pipes and Walker 1979) employed this methodology. Following this methodology, however, gives rise to a variety of problems. First, only the first-round effects of the excise tax are incorporated and, hence, the actual distribution of the tax burden may differ substantially from the estimate. Second, this method may not even provide good estimates of the first-round effects of the tax because the relative burden of a particular tax borne by a family is determined not by the family's consumption of the taxed item but by the fraction of the family's income spent on the item relative to the national average.

In view of these problems with the traditional approach, and given that the proportions of income spent on different items by various income groups do not vary widely from the average, we decided for the purposes of this study to distribute excise taxes in the same way as general sales taxes; that is to say, this study assumes that excise taxes burden total incomes—excluding government transfers to persons.

So, the answer to the question, "Who pays the indirect taxes?" is ultimately a straightforward one. Although indirect taxes appear in a variety of forms, they burden the income that the family earns.

Other taxes by other names

In addition to "formal" taxes levied by government, there are a variety of other government policies that have the same effect as taxes but are not normally identified as such: the regulations that restrict our activities every day, price support for producers of agricultural products, and import duties and quotas to assist clothing and textile manufacturers. There is no difference in principle between this sort of tax and other hidden taxes. These "taxes" do not show up in records of government revenue and precise estimates of their size are difficult to make but we cannot ignore their existence.

Regulatory taxation

In general, a government can achieve a given objective either by taxation and subsidization or by regulation. Rather than the current practice of imposing import quotas to help Canadian clothing manufacturers, the federal government could provide assistance by giving them a direct subsidy financed from general tax revenue. That the government uses regulation to convey the subsidy should not distract from the fact that a subsidy is being provided and that it is the Canadian consumer who is paying for it.

For governments, regulation seems a painless way of advancing their public policy without spending tax dollars directly. The reality of regulation is not so benign since it increases the cost of doing business. Governments bear little of the cost of regulation: their costs are limited to the administrative share while businesses and consumers must bear the much larger cost of complying with the regulations.

According to a recent study by The Fraser Institute, the compliance cost of all federal, provincial, and municipal regulations amounted to $103 billion in 1997/1998 (Jones and Graf 2001). This works out to $13,700 per family of four. The federal and provincial governments legislated over 117,000 regulations over the 24-year period investigated in the study; the federal government alone passed an average of 1,042 regulations per year. "Regulation affects almost every aspect of our lives, including what we listen to on the radio, the prices and quality of the food we eat, the safety features in our cars, who is allowed to deliver our mail, where we are permitted to smoke and drink, and how we are restricted in the use of our property." (Jones and Graf 2001:3)

Marketing-board taxes

There are dozens of cartels controlling farm products in Canada. These cartels or marketing boards generally have the effect of suppressing competition in the production of the product subject to the cartel and, consequently, they cause the price of the product to be higher than it would otherwise have been. The amount by which the marketing board price exceeds the price that would prevail in its absence—that is, in the open market—is a tax on the consumer and marketing boards ought to be viewed as a device for transferring money from consumers to producers.

The Organisation for Economic Co-operation and Development (OECD) estimates that the implicit tax in the form of support for the market prices of agricultural products paid by Canadian consumers was $3.0 billion in 2001. Total household spending on food in Canada is roughly $75.7 billion; marketing boards and other implicit agricultural taxes add about $252 (3.9%) to the cost of the average family's food bill.

Canada and the OECD countries adopted a set of principles for agricultural policy reform in 1987. Since then, there has been a decrease in support to the agricultural sector although the OECD notes that there has been only "modest progress in agricultural policy reform since the mid-80s." and "the continued dominance of the most distorting forms of support means that farmers remain shielded from world market signals. The current support levels impose a burden on consumers and taxpayers" (OECD 2002b: 10). In general, Canada's implementation of these reforms since 1987 has included a shift away from supporting market prices towards making direct payments to producers. The exception is in the dairy industry, Canada's most heavily supported and least reformed agricultural sector, which receives over 35% of total producer support and almost 75% of the dollar value of market-price support from consumers: "the dairy sector stands out as one [sector] where there has been no progress towards market orientation" (OECD 2002b: 84).

Due to trade liberalization and internal reforms, the level of agricultural support in OECD countries is lower than in 1987 and this means lower implicit taxes for Canadians. If the reform process continues and, especially if the Canadian dairy sector is reformed, Canadian consumers will experience a further reduction in implicit taxes caused by government support of market prices.

Clothing and textile taxes

In November 1976, the federal government imposed a quota on imported clothing and textiles. Its purpose was to limit the importation of inexpensive clothing and textiles and so protect Canadian clothing and textile manufacturers from competition. The associated decline in competition for the Canadian consumer's clothing-expenditure dollar undoubtedly produced a higher price for clothing than would otherwise have existed. The difference between the price for clothing that would have prevailed in the absence of the quota and the price that actually prevails is a tax on the consumer. Proceeds from this tax go directly to producers who are, in effect, being subsidized by the consumers.

Some of the burden associated with tariffs and quotas has been eliminated as a result of the North American Free Trade Agreement (NAFTA) between Canada, the United States, and Mexico. However, in many cases the principal source of cheaper products is not the United States but less developed countries. In value terms, 77.4% of textile imports into Canada come from developed countries while 71.5% of clothing imports come from developing countries (Canadian Textiles Institute, personal communication to Joel Emes, 1998).

The authors of Free Trade between the United States and Canada estimated that the total amount of tax levied in the form of tariff protection or other barriers to international competition was as high as 10.5% of Canada's Gross National Product (Wonnacott and Wonnacott 1967: 299). More recent studies estimated the costs of tariffs at 8.2% of GDP in 1974 (Wonnacott 1975) and 8.6% of GDP in 1976 (Harris and Cox 1983). Canada has seen a significant reduction in tariff protection since these studies were completed. In 1981, import duties were equal to 3.6% of imports from other countries, by 1991 they were only 2.3%, and by 2002 they were down to 0.8%. However, a recent report by the World Trade Organization indicates concerns about market access for developing countries in certain areas of agriculture and textiles and clothing (World Trade Organization 2003), indicating that Canada continues to impose these hidden taxes on consumers.

Deferred taxation

During his budget statement in November 1978, the Honourable Jean Chrétien, then Federal Minister of Finance, made much of the fact that, because the personal income tax structure had been indexed to inflation, there had, in effect, been a reduction in personal income taxation compared to what would have prevailed in the absence of indexing. That is to say, exemptions had been increased by the rate of inflation and tax brackets had been shifted to ensure that incomes swollen by inflation would not be taxed more heavily on that account alone. While this change in the tax structure was indeed welcome, it did not represent a move towards a permanent reduction in the government's propensity to tax.

The "reduction" in personal income-tax revenues, in fact, was accompanied—starting in 1975—by deficits in the federal government's accounts that were unprecedented in peacetime. Although this situation is not entirely attributable to the relative decline in personal income-tax revenues, it is clear that continued growth in income taxation would have meant a smaller deficit and a reduction in net cash requirements to be financed by issuing debt.

Accordingly, it has been standard practice in assessing Canada's current level of taxation to take into account the extent to which tax collections are merely deferred by current tax "reductions." In other words, in addition to calculating the total tax burden of all government operations in a given year, we have in the past calculated the balanced-budget tax burden, which included not only taxes levied now but also taxes that must be levied in the future to discharge debts acquired by the government to finance the current deficit. In recent years, there has been a dramatic shift away from deficit financing, or deferred taxation, in favour of balanced or surplus budgets. This shift has made the continued calculation of a balanced-budget tax burden unnecessary. Nevertheless, the historical balanced-budget tax burden and the effect of debt repayment on the tax burden are discussed in chapter 4.

How much tax should Canadians pay?

In 1917, when he first introduced the Personal Income Tax, the Finance Minister, Sir Thomas White, was of the opinion that no Canadian should pay tax on income less than $2,000 if he were single and had no dependents. Married taxpayers, he said, should pay tax on income in excess of $3,000. The tax structure that ultimately evolved provided that single Canadians paid income tax on income in excess of $1,500, while married Canadians were exempted from the tax until their incomes exceeded $3,000. However, in the very next year, this was reduced to $2,000 for a married taxpayer and $1,000 for single Canadians (Government of Canada 1917).

While the tax structure has gone through many changes in the intervening years, it is interesting to ask how Canadians would be taxed if this initial view of the "ability to pay" had kept pace with developments in people's incomes. To answer this question we have adjusted the original exemption levels by the increase in inflation over the period since 1917. This adjustment yields an exemption level for 2003 of $19,492 for single taxpayers and $38,984 for married taxpayers. But actual personal credits for single and married taxpayers amounted to $7,756 and $14,342 in 2003—significantly less than the level of income that would have been exempt if the 1917 standard had continued in force. The reason for the disparity is that, over the years from 1917 to 1974, exemption levels were not indexed to the cost of living or the increase in family incomes—in fact, in a few years during the Depression, exemption levels were actually reduced. In addition, exemption levels and tax brackets were only partially indexed to inflation between 1986 and 1999.

Chapter 2
Personal Income Taxation in Canada

PERSONAL INCOME TAX IS THE LARGEST SINGLE SOURCE of government revenue. It follows, therefore, that the largest single tax paid by the average Canadian family is the income tax. This tax came into existence in 1917 as a "temporary" emergency measure to help finance the increasing debt incurred during World War I. Nothing, it seems, endures like the temporary.

The current income tax structure
Several significant changes to personal income taxation were announced or confirmed in 1999 and 2000. These changes include the re-indexation of exemptions and brackets and the move by the provinces from "tax-on-tax" assessment of personal income to "tax-on-income" assessment.

Bracket creep
Many Canadian taxpayers have been pushed into higher tax brackets and have seen the value of their basic exemption eroded in recent years because governments have not always adjusted brackets and exemptions to mitigate the effects of inflation. The best way to illustrate this problem, which is often called "bracket creep," is with an example. If a worker earning $29,000 in 2000 received a 5% raise to compensate for a 5% increase in prices, her income would increase to $30,450. This 5% raise

would almost allow her to maintain her standard of living but falls short because she would now pay more income tax relative to her income than when she earned $29,000. Whereas all of the $29,000 was taxed at the 17% federal rate, the part of $30,450 in excess of $29,000 is taxed at the 25% federal rate. In the 2000 budget, the federal government announced that it would index all brackets and exemptions to the inflation rate for the 2001 and subsequent taxation years, thus ending bracket creep in the federal personal income-tax system.

Tax-on-tax assessment and tax-on-income assessment

The federal and provincial governments share personal income taxation. Prior to 2000, most provinces based their personal income tax on the "basic federal tax." Residents of provinces other than Quebec determined their basic tax owing by multiplying the basic federal tax by the provincial tax rate; hence the term "tax-on-tax" applied to most of the provincial personal income-tax systems. Quebec has operated its own personal income-tax system since 1954 on the "tax-on-income" basis. Tax-on-income assessment parallels the federal personal income-tax calculation, with taxable income as the starting point for the tax calculation. British Columbia, Manitoba, New Brunswick, Nova Scotia, and Ontario introduced tax-on-income systems in 2000. Alberta, Saskatchewan, Prince Edward Island, Newfoundland and Labrador, and the territories introduced tax-on-income systems for 2001. Tax-on-income assessment gives the provincial governments more flexibility in changing their personal income-tax systems to suit the needs and priorities of their constituents. The switch to tax-on-income also protects provincial revenues from decreases in federal personal income tax that, in a tax-on-tax system, automatically translate into decreases in provincial personal income tax because they decrease the basic federal tax and, therefore, the base for the provincial tax calculation. For a good overview of the recent changes to the provincial personal income tax systems, see Ort and Perry (2000) and Treff and Perry (1999).

Combined income-tax rates

Table 2.1 presents the actual income-tax rates (combined federal and provincial) encountered by the average single individual at various levels of taxable income in 1992 through 2003. As the figures show, the minimum rate of tax in 2003 is 23.68%, payable on the range of taxable income from $1.00 to $32,183. The second rate is 32.56%, payable on the range of

Table 2.1: Combined federal and provincial personal income tax rates, 1992–2003

1992		1995		2000		2003	
Taxable income	Rate (%)	Taxable income	Rate (%)	Taxable income	Rate (%)	Taxable income	Rate (%)
$1–$29,590	26.61	$1–$29,590	26.35	$1–$30,004	25.16	$1–$32,183	23.68
$29,591–$59,180	40.69	$29,591–$59,180	40.30	$30,005–$60,009	37.00	$32,184–$64,368	32.56
$59,181–$62,192	45.39	$59,181–$62,192	44.95	$60,010–$74,240	42.92	$64,369–$104,648	38.48
$62,193 & above	46.84	$62,193 & above	46.40	$74,241 & above	44.37	$104,649 & above	42.92

Sources: Canadian Tax Foundation, *The National Finances* 1993 and 1994; *Finances of The Nation* 1995 through 2002; federal and provincial budgets; calculations by the authors.

taxable income from $32,184 to $64,368. The third rate is 38.48%, payable on the range of taxable income from $64,369 to $104,648. The maximum rate of 42.92% is payable on taxable income in excess of $104,649. These rates are the marginal rates of tax encountered as one moves from one level of taxable income to the next. Table 2.2 shows the combined federal and provincial marginal tax rates for a single individual in each province at three levels of income. An equally interesting series of calculations shows the amount of tax an individual pays on a given amount of total, rather than taxable, income (see table 2.3).

The situation can be slightly different for families because there are credits permitted for the dependent spouse. Support of children also eases somewhat the tax burden on the taxpayer. In perusing tax rates for the average family of four presented in table 2.4, the reader should bear in mind that this schedule of rates is not applicable to all families. In many cases, both adult members of the family declare taxable income and, since each files a separate return, tax rates for individuals apply. Of course, this is to the advantage of the taxpayers. If, for example, a childless couple who are both working have the same income—say $25,000 per year—they pay total tax of about $8,224 when they file as individuals. If the family's total income of $50,000 were earned by only one of them, the total tax payable would be about $10,124—a difference of $1,900. In other words, if the family's income is earned by one family member, the

Table 2.2: Personal income tax for a single taxpayer, combined federal and provincial marginal rates (%), 2002

	Income		
	$20,000	$50,000	$100,000
Newfoundland	24.7	38.2	45.6
Prince Edward Island	24.0	35.8	44.4
Nova Scotia	29.0	37.0	44.3
New Brunswick	23.9	36.8	42.5
Quebec	27.1	38.4	45.7
Ontario	20.5	31.2	43.4
Manitoba	26.0	37.4	43.4
Saskatchewan	25.4	35.3	41.5
Alberta	24.2	32.0	36.0
British Columbia	20.5	31.2	40.7

Source: Canadian Tax Foundation, *Finances of The Nation 2002*.

Table 2.3: Combined federal and provincial personal income tax and tax rate (single taxpayer with no dependants), 2002

Total income ($)	Total tax payable ($)	Rate (%)
7,500	0	0.0
10,000	560	5.6
12,500	1,152	9.2
15,000	1,744	11.6
17,500	2,336	13.3
20,000	2,928	14.6
25,000	4,112	16.4
30,000	5,296	17.7
50,000	11,659	23.3
100,000	30,108	30.1
200,000	72,895	36.4

Sources: Provincial budgets and tax forms; calculations by the authors.

family pays a gross tax rate of 20.2% but, if this income is composed of two salaries, the tax rate is only 16.4%. The difference between the two tax rates rises as family income increases until very high income levels are reached (see table 2.5). This difference between the tax rates of families with a single income and those with double incomes affects many of the

Table 2.4: Combined federal & provincial personal income tax, Canada Child Tax Benefit, and tax rate (married taxpayer with two dependent children under 16), 2002

Total income ($)	Total tax payable ($)	Canada Child Tax Benefit ($)	Net tax ($)	Rate (%)
15,000	209	4,613	(4,404)	(29.4)
17,500	801	4,613	(3,812)	(21.8)
20,000	1,393	4,613	(3,220)	(16.1)
25,000	2,577	4,534	(1,957)	(7.8)
30,000	3,761	3,675	86	0.3
50,000	10,124	1,898	8,226	16.5
100,000	28,573	321	28,252	28.3
200,000	71,360	0	71,360	35.7

Sources: Provincial budgets, tax forms, Canada Customs and Revenue Agency; calculations by the authors.

Table 2.5: Tax rates for a married couple, 2002

Total family income ($)	One income earner		Two income earners	
	Tax ($)	Tax rate (%)	Tax ($)	Tax rate (%)
15,000	209	1.4	0	0.0
20,000	1,393	7.0	1,120	5.6
25,000	2,577	10.3	2,304	9.2
30,000	3,761	12.5	3,488	11.6
50,000	10,124	20.2	8,224	16.4
100,000	28,573	28.6	23,318	23.3
200,000	71,360	35.7	60,216	30.1

Sources: Provincial budgets and tax forms; calculations by the authors.

other calculations in the remainder of this book. In particular, income-tax payments shown in the various composite tax tables in chapter 3 reflect the fact that, on average, tax payments are made by a mixture of single-taxpayer and double-taxpayer families.

Who pays the income tax bill?

According to data for 2001 from the Canada Customs and Revenue Agency (formerly Revenue Canada), a total of $112.5 billion in income taxes was paid by individuals and, as table 2.6 shows, 32.8% was paid

Table 2.6: Income, taxes, and tax returns filed, by income group,

Income group by total income assessed ($000s)	Percentage of total tax paid by this income group	Percentage of total tax paid by all groups at or below this income group	Percentage of total returns filed by this income group
loss or nil	0.0	0.0	1.4
.001–10	0.1	0.1	22.3
10–15	0.8	1.0	13.1
15–20	2.0	2.9	9.8
20–25	3.1	6.1	7.9
25–30	4.3	10.3	7.4
30–35	5.2	15.6	6.8
35–40	5.7	21.3	5.7
40–45	5.9	27.1	4.8
45–50	5.7	32.8	3.8
50–60	10.7	43.5	5.8
60–70	9.1	52.6	3.9
70–80	6.7	59.3	2.3
80–90	4.8	64.1	1.4
90–100	3.6	67.7	0.9
100–150	9.4	77.1	1.7
150–250	7.1	84.2	0.7
250+	15.8	100.0	0.4

Sources: Revenue Canada, *Income Statistics 2003–2001 Tax Year*; calculations by the authors.

by individuals with incomes below $50,000. Individuals with incomes below $60,000 paid 43.5% of the total income tax bill. In fact, 29.9% of all income taxes were paid by individuals with yearly incomes in the relatively narrow range of $20,000 to $50,000.

As column 5 of table 2.6 shows, nearly one-half of all returns were filed by individuals with incomes less than $20,000. This proportion reflects the large number of part-time workers, students employed during the summer, and other intermittent workers earning low incomes. These taxpayers generated only 2.9% of total tax revenue, while the top 31.4% of taxpayers—those declaring income of $35,000 or more—contributed 84.4% of the total income tax bill.

An interesting aspect of the information in table 2.6 is the relation between taxes paid and income declared. For example, while 15.6% of the total income-tax bill was paid by individuals with incomes below $35,000,

2001 tax year

Percentage of total returns filed by all groups at or below this income group	Percentage of total income declared by this income group	Percentage of total income declared by all groups at or below this income group
1.4	(0.1)	(0.1)
23.7	3.5	3.4
36.8	5.2	8.6
46.6	5.4	13.9
54.5	5.6	19.5
61.9	6.4	26.0
68.6	6.9	32.9
74.3	6.8	39.7
79.1	6.4	46.0
82.9	5.8	51.8
88.7	10.0	61.8
92.6	8.0	69.8
94.9	5.4	75.2
96.3	3.7	78.9
97.2	2.6	81.6
98.9	6.3	87.9
99.6	4.2	92.1
100.0	7.9	100.0

column 6 reveals that this group earned 32.9% of all the income declared. So, those earning incomes below $35,000 paid a smaller proportion of the total tax bill than their share of total earned income might suggest. On the other hand, the top 31.4% of taxpayers, those who had incomes in excess of $35,000, paid about 84.4% of the total tax bill, while receiving only 67.1% of total income earned.

The reason for this, of course, is that the income-tax structure is "progressive." That is, it takes a larger fraction from high incomes than it does from low incomes, as is clear from the tax rates presented in table 2.4. Sales taxes also contribute to progressivity, even though everyone pays the same rate irrespective of income, because sales-tax rebates vary inversely with income. Furthermore, many income transfers from the state are indexed to the price of goods so that, as the price rises due to a sales tax, so do the transfers. This eases the burden of sales taxes to the poor.

Chapter 3
How Much Tax Do
You Really Pay?

WHILE INCOME TAX IS THE SINGLE LARGEST TAX CATEGORY, it represents less than half of the total taxes paid by the average Canadian family. The purpose of this chapter is to expand the discussion to include all taxes that Canadians pay.

How much income do you really earn?
Cash income
In order to calculate properly how much tax a person or group pays, it is necessary first to determine income. This is a complex calculation because there are a multitude of sources of income other than wages and salaries. This chapter explains the method for deriving the income figures used in subsequent sections.

The ultimate goal of income calculations is to determine the total income a Canadian citizen would have if there were no taxes of any sort and other factors remained unchanged. To arrive at such a figure, it is necessary to determine all the sources of income a person might have and all of the taxes that would have been paid on this income before the person received it. The first layer of sources is easily discovered: wages, salaries, interest from savings bonds, or rent from the in-law suite in the basement are the sorts of items that make up cash income.

Cash income and under-reporting

In its regular surveys of household income, Statistics Canada finds that people typically omit some income items when they estimate their cash income. That is, they under-report their income. The particular items omitted vary from family to family but, on average, families tend to underestimate their total income by 4% to 12%. Items that might be omitted include miscellaneous interest income, income from "moonlighting," and so on. Fortunately, Statistics Canada does have a comprehensive measure of income in the National Accounts framework, upon which estimates of cash income used in this study are based.

It may be useful at this stage to provide an example based on a fictitious family. In order to make the example as comprehensive as possible, it is assumed that the family has income from all of the sources identified in the study—an unlikely circumstance for any real family. The example is presented in table 3.1.

Total income

In addition to cash income, most families also have various forms of non-cash income that must be included in a comprehensive income figure. For example, most wage and salary earners receive fringe benefits as a condition of their employment and their income also includes the investment income accumulated by their pension plan and the interest accumulated—though not paid—on their insurance policies.

At a higher level of subtlety, a comprehensive income total should also include a number of other income sources. For example, income must

Table 3.1: Cash income, 2003

Wages & salaries	$41,134
Income from farm operations	150
Unincorporated non-farm income	2,677
Interest	1,703
Dividends	661
Private and government pension payments	3,657
Old age pension payments	1,715
Other transfers from government	7,085
Cash income	$58,782

Source: The Fraser Institute's Canadian Tax Simulator 2003.

be imputed on account of interest-free loans that people make. The interest foregone is, in fact, implicit income in the form of a gift.

Profits not paid out as dividends by corporations but held in the form of retained earnings are income of the shareholders of the corporation, even though they do not receive it in the year in which it is reported. Finally, food consumed by farm operators is evaluated at market price and attributed to farm operators as income.

Again, to make the calculation clear, the accumulated total income is shown in table 3.2 for a fictitious family that is assumed to have income from all sources.

Total income before tax

Some of the income earned by Canadians is taxed before they receive it. For example, shareholders receive dividends on corporate profits after corporate profit taxes have been paid. In the absence of taxes, the dividends or retained earnings of the shareholder would have been higher. Therefore, in order to arrive at total income before tax, it is necessary to add the tax on corporate profits collected from corporations. Similarly, if there were no property taxes, net after-tax rental income would be higher than it actually is. Therefore, before-tax income must be augmented by the amount of property taxes paid.

Indirect and hidden taxes reduce the effective income available to Canadians because they increase the prices of items that people buy with their incomes. In effect, income after tax is less, in terms of what it will buy, than it was before the tax. In order to arrive at an estimate of income before tax it is necessary to add to incomes the reduction brought about

Table 3.2: Total income, 2003

Cash income	$58,782
Fringe benefits from employment	7,637
Investment income from insurance companies	883
Investment income from pension plans	2,461
Imputed interest	351
Value of food from farms	11
Corporate retained earnings	2,623
Total income	$72,748

Source: The Fraser Institute's Canadian Tax Simulator 2003.

by indirect taxes. Payroll taxes levied on firms are, as noted earlier, effectively paid by employees, because the taxes reduce the amount of money available to pay wages and salaries. Accordingly, it is necessary to add the amount of payroll taxes to employees' incomes to arrive at an estimate of total income before tax.

Table 3.3 presents an example of a complete income calculation for a fictitious family that is assumed to have income from all of the income sources identified in the study and to have paid all of the identified taxes.

Calculating the total tax bill

The tax calculation for the average Canadian family consists of adding up the various taxes that the family pays. Hidden taxes, such as taxes on tobacco and alcohol, are allocated according to the method described

Table 3.3: Total income before tax, 2003

Wages & salaries	$41,134
Income from farm operations	150
Unincorporated non-farm income	2,677
Interest	1,703
Dividends	661
Private and government pension payments	3,657
Old age pension payments	1,715
Other transfers from government	7,085
Cash income	$58,782
Plus	
Fringe benefits from employment	7,637
Investment income from insurance companies	883
Investment income from pension plans	2,461
Imputed interest	351
Value of food from farms	11
Corporate retained earnings	2,623
Total income	$72,748
Plus	
Property taxes	2,375
Profit taxes	2,556
Indirect taxes	12,779
Total income before tax	$90,458

Source: The Fraser Institute's Canadian Tax Simulator 2003.

in chapter 1. To preserve consistency, the family used for the example of the tax calculation in table 3.4 is the same family used in the income calculation.

A note on the calculation of Tax Freedom Day

The calculations in this chapter underlie our calculation of Tax Freedom Day, the day of the year when the average family has earned enough income to pay the total tax bill imposed on it by all levels of government. We are occasionally asked why we calculate Tax Freedom Day using cash income rather than total income before tax. We use cash income because the main purpose of Tax Freedom Day is to convey the size of the total tax bill imposed on Canadian families in a format that is easily understood. If we told people that taxes are 31% of their total income before tax, they would have a large task ahead of them to estimate all the types of income that must be included to arrive at this measure of income. Many people think of cash income (wages and salaries, government transfers, pension payments, interest and dividends, farm income, and self-employment income) as their total income. Most do not consider all the other types of

---

Table 3.4: Tax bill of the average Canadian family, 2003

Total cash income	$58,782
Total income before tax	90,458
Taxes	
Income taxes	8,887
Sales taxes	4,507
Liquor, tobacco, amusement & other excise taxes	1,772
Automobile, fuel & motor-vehicle licence taxes	733
Social security, medical & hospital taxes	5,659
Property taxes	2,375
Import duties	241
Profits tax	2,556
Natural resource taxes	333
Other taxes	578
Total taxes	27,640
Taxes as a percentage of total cash income	47%
Taxes as a percentage of total income before tax	31%

Source: The Fraser Institute's Canadian Tax Simulator 2003.

income they earn but do not see (including corporate retained earnings, the investment income on their pension plans, and indirect taxes) as part of their total income. For example, if we were to report that the total tax burden for the average family was 31% most people with a family cash income of $58,000 would estimate their tax bill at $17,980 when it is actually closer to $27,000. The crucial piece of information is that governments extracted $27,000 from your family; the particular definition of income is secondary. Cash income is a useful tool in describing the tax burden because it does not force people to go through arithmetic gymnastics to arrive at their total income before tax to get an idea of how large the total tax burden is.

Chapter 4
The Canadian Consumer Tax Index and Tax Freedom Day

IT IS ALWAYS SATISFYING TO FIND ONE NUMBER, or index, that neatly summarizes a complicated issue. It is seldom the case that such a number exists. IQ scores, for instance, do not say everything about an individual's intelligence and the speed of a computer chip can only give a rough idea of how that computer will perform. The same is true of Canadian taxes. Our system is complex and there is no single number that can give us a complete idea of who pays how much, and how the system has changed over time. That said, we can introduce two of the better indicators of the state of the tax burden of the average Canadian family: the Canadian Consumer Tax Index and Tax Freedom Day.

The Canadian Consumer Tax Index

For individual taxpayers, the most interesting variable is how much tax they actually have to pay. In The Fraser Institute's first tax study, How Much Tax Do You Really Pay? (Walker 1976b), we devised an index that we called the Canadian Consumer Tax Index (CCTI). Its purpose was to provide a summary-at-a-glance of what has been happening to the tax bill faced by the average Canadian family over the years since 1961.

Some readers of that book found the tax index too simple—it failed to take into account how the tax money was spent by governments and, therefore, showed only one side of the ledger (McGillivray 1976). In our analyses, revenue collection and government spending are considered separately because they are distinct government actions. Government spending is considered in various publications including Government Spending Facts 2 (Horry and Walker 1994), and our government report cards (Law, Markowitz and Mihlar 1997; Boucher 1998; Chera and Mihlar 1998; Clemens and Emes 2001; Clemens et al. 2003). Further, the index in that first study and in all subsequent studies has been widely used by financial and consumer affairs columnists across the country to describe how the Canadian tax system has evolved. Moreover, it has been in continuous use ever since its release and has been described as the most up-to-date measure of the extent of Canadian taxation.

What is the Canadian Consumer Tax Index?

The Canadian Consumer Tax Index tracks the total tax bill paid by a Canadian family with average income. The "consumer" in question is the taxpaying family, which can be thought of as consuming government services. The Consumer Price Index measures the average price that consumers pay for the goods and services that they buy of their own choice. The CCTI measures the price of goods and services that government buys on behalf of its constituents (see table 4.1 and figure 4.1).

The CCTI is constructed by calculating the difference in the tax bill of an average Canadian family from the tax bill in the base year of 1961 for each of the years included in the index. Now, while each of these families had average income in the year selected, the family is not the same one from year to year. The objective is not to trace the tax experience of a particular family but rather to plot the experience of a family that was average in each year.

The CCTI thus answers the following question: How has the tax burden of the average family changed since 1961, bearing in mind that

Table 4.1: The Canadian Consumer Tax Index (1961 = 100)

1961	100	1985	886	1998	1,356
1969	186	1990	1,116	2000	1,556
1974	324	1992	1,111	2002	1,594
1976	357	1994	1,173	2003	1,650
1981	682	1996	1,263		

Source: The Fraser Institute's Canadian Tax Simulator 2003.

Figure 4.1: The Canadian Consumer Tax Index, 1961–2003

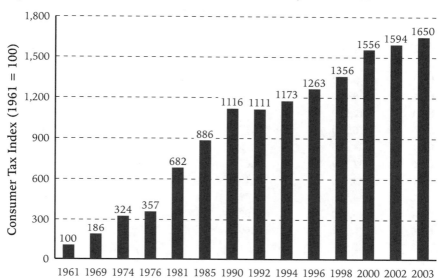

Source: Table 4.1.

the average family has itself changed in that period? We can note, for example, that the average family in 2003 is headed by an older person, one who is more likely to own a car and a house, and has fewer members than the average family in 1961 (see Dominion Bureau of Statistics 1962 and Statistics Canada 1983 and 2002). Most important, the family's earned income increased by 1,076% over the period.

The basis of the CCTI is the total tax calculation presented in the "Tax Bill" column of table 4.2. Calculations of income and tax were made for a selection of years beginning in 1961 and ending in 2003. The results show that the tax bill of the average Canadian family has increased by 1,550% from 1961 and that the index has a value of 1,650 for 2003 (see table 4.5).

Part of that increase reflects the effects of inflation. In order to eliminate the portion of the increase due to the erosion of purchasing power, we have also calculated the tax index in real dollars—that is, dollars of 2003 purchasing power. While this adjustment has the effect of reducing the steepness of the index's path over time, the real-dollar tax index, nevertheless, increased by 152.6% over the period (see table 4.3).

Table 4.2: Taxes paid by the average Canadian family (families and unattached individuals), 1961–2003

	Average cash income ($)	Total income before tax ($)	Tax bill ($)	Increase in tax bill over base year (%)
1961	5,000	7,582	1,675	—
1969	8,000	11,323	3,117	86
1974	12,500	17,976	5,429	224
1976	16,500	21,872	5,979	257
1981	27,980	38,758	11,429	582
1985	32,309	46,451	14,834	786
1990	43,170	60,195	18,693	1,016
1992	44,246	62,791	18,602	1,011
1994	44,720	65,993	19,647	1,073
1996	45,932	68,604	21,148	1,163
1998	48,908	72,193	22,713	1,256
2000	54,283	82,027	26,068	1,456
2002	57,492	86,288	26,696	1,494
2003	58,782	90,458	27,640	1,550

Source: The Fraser Institute's Canadian Tax Simulator 2003.

Table 4.3: Inflation-adjusted tax bill and Consumer Tax Index, 1961–2003

	Tax bill (2003 $)	Percent change in taxes since 1961
1961	10,941	—
1969	16,271	48.7
1974	21,323	94.9
1976	19,686	79.9
1981	23,703	116.6
1985	24,160	120.8
1990	24,473	123.7
1992	22,722	107.7
1994	23,528	115.0
1996	24,393	122.9
1998	25,547	133.5
2000	28,055	156.4
2002	27,402	150.5
2003	27,640	152.6

Sources: The Fraser Institute's Canadian Tax Simulator 2003; Statistics Canada, The Consumer Price Index, catalogue 62-001-XPB.

What the Canadian Consumer Tax Index shows

The dramatic increase in the CCTI over the period from 1961 to 2003 was produced by the interaction of a number of factors. First, there was a dramatic increase in incomes over the period and, even with no change in tax rates, the family's tax bill would have increased substantially: growth in family income alone would have produced an increase in the tax bill from $1,675 in 1961 to $19,692 in 2003. The second contributing factor was a 40.4% increase in the tax rate faced by the average family.

The increase in the tax burden is even greater when deferred taxation, in the form of deficit financing, is included. Figure 4.2 shows what the CCTI looks like when the annual deficits of governments are added to the tax bill. From the mid-1970s until recently, federal and provincial governments resorted to issuing debt to finance a significant portion of their expenditures. Politicians seem finally to have recovered from their infatuation with this form of taxation as the federal government and a half of the provincial governments announced balanced budgets for 2003/2004. In addition, the federal government and the provinces as a whole posted a surplus in 2002/2003.

Figure 4.2: The Balanced Budget Tax Index, 1961–2003

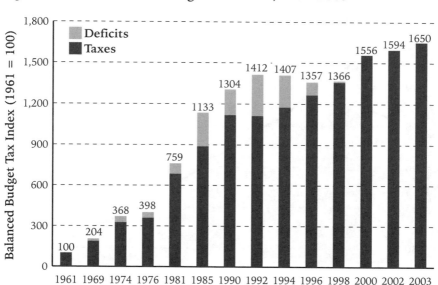

Source: The Fraser Institute's Canadian Tax Simulator 2003.

What if we got rid of the debt?

A deficit is the amount that government must borrow in any given year to finance spending in excess of revenue. Over the years, these deficits accumulate. This accumulation is known as the debt. All debt must one day be paid off, either by increased taxes or reduced services. There is simply no getting around this fact. Getting rid of deficits is not the same as getting rid of the debt. How would the average Canadian family's tax burden change if all levels of government decided to eliminate their debts by the year 2023? Assuming a favourable growth rate for real income of 4%, population growth of 0.8%, and no change in government spending per capita, the average Canadian family's tax bill would rise by $3,463 in the first year to pay off the debt within 20 years. The average family's tax rate would jump from 47.0% in 2003 to 52.9% in 2004 and gradually fall to 28.3% in 2023 as seen in figure 4.3.

Taxes versus the necessities of life

While the CCTI shows how the average family's tax bill has changed over the past 42 years, that information becomes even more significant when it

---

Figure 4.3: The impact of gross government debt repayment on the average Canadian family, 2002–2023

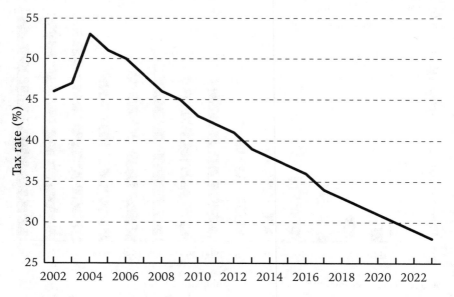

Source: Statistics Canada; 2003 Federal Budget; calculations by the authors.

is compared with other major expenditures of the average Canadian family for shelter, food, and clothing.

Table 4.4 compares the average dollar amount of family cash income, total income before tax, and total taxes paid with family expenditures on shelter, food, and clothing. Figure 4.4 compares the tax bill to spending on basic needs. It is clear from these figures that taxation has not only become the most significant item that consumers face in their budgets but that it is also growing more rapidly than any other single item. This is made more evident in table 4.5 and figure 4.5, which show the various items as indices based on 1961 values. Total income before tax rose by 1,093% during the period from 1961 to 2003, prices rose by 553%, expenditures on shelter by 936%, food by 460%, and clothing by 416%. Meanwhile, the tax bill of the average family grew by 1,550%.

Table 4.4: Income, taxes, and selected expenditures of the average Canadian family (dollars)

	Average cash income	Total income before tax	Average tax bill	Average expenditures*		
				Shelter**	Food	Clothing
1961	5,000	7,582	1,675	1,130	1,259	435
1969	8,000	11,323	3,117	1,497	1,634	654
1974	12,500	17,976	5,429	2,294	2,320	886
1976	16,500	21,872	5,979	3,134	2,838	1,119
1981	27,980	38,758	11,429	5,381	4,440	1,499
1985	32,309	46,451	14,834	6,984	4,899	2,141
1990	43,170	60,195	18,693	8,776	5,745	2,234
1992	44,246	62,791	18,602	9,607	6,024	2,215
1994	44,720	65,993	19,647	9,592	6,066	2,116
1996	45,932	68,604	21,148	9,577	6,108	2,017
1998	48,908	72,193	22,713	10,253	6,048	2,142
2000	54,283	82,027	26,068	10,630	6,318	2,152
2002	57,492	86,288	26,696	11,392	6,911	2,294
2003	58,782	90,458	27,640	11,715	7,045	2,245

Sources: Statistics Canada, Urban Family Expenditure, catalogue 62-549, 62-547, 62-544, 62-537, 62-535, 62-541, 62-525, 62-555; 1990, 1992, and 1996 Family Expenditure Surveys, catalogue 62-555; 1998 and 2001 Survey of Household Spending; The Consumer Price Index, 62-001-XPB; The Fraser Institute's Canadian Tax Simulator 2003.
* All expenditure items include indirect taxes. ** Average Shelter Expenditures for years prior to 1998 are estimates. The estimate is to take account of a change in the definition of shelter between the Family Expenditure Survey and the Survey of Household Expenditures.

Figure 4.4: Taxes and basic expenditures* of the average Canadian family, 1961–2003

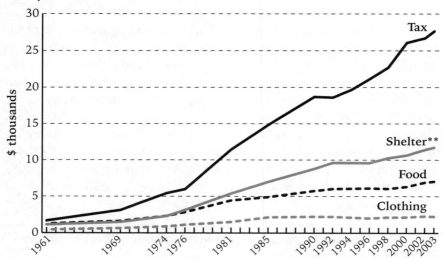

Source: Table 4.4; data for some years have been interpolated. * All expenditure items include indirect taxes; ** measurement of shelter has changed; see note to table 4.4 for more information.

Figure 4.5: How the Canadian Consumer Tax Index has increased relative to other indices, 1961–2003

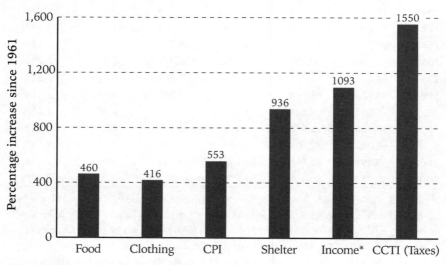

Source: Table 4.5. * Total income before tax.

Table 4.5: Income, tax, and expenditure indices (1961 = 100)

	Income		Tax	Consumer Prices	Average expenditures*		
	Average cash income	Total income before tax	Consumer Tax Index	Average CPI	Shelter	Food	Clothing
1961	100	100	100	100	100	100	100
1969	160	149	186	125	132	130	150
1974	250	237	324	166	203	184	204
1976	330	288	357	198	277	225	257
1981	560	511	682	315	476	353	345
1985	646	613	886	401	618	389	492
1990	863	794	1,116	499	776	456	514
1992	885	828	1,111	535	850	478	509
1994	894	870	1,173	545	849	482	486
1996	919	905	1,263	566	847	485	464
1998	978	952	1,356	581	907	480	492
2000	1,086	1,082	1,556	607	940	502	495
2002	1,150	1,138	1,594	636	1,008	549	527
2003	1,176	1,193	1,650	653	1,036	560	516

Percentage increase 1961–2003

	1,076	1,093	1,550	553	936	460	416

Sources: Table 4.5; The Fraser Institute's Canadian Tax Simulator 2003.
Note: All figures in this table are converted to indices by dividing each series in table 4.4 by its value in 1961, and then multiplying that figure by 100.
* All expenditure items include indirect taxes.

Table 4.6 and figure 4.6 present the same information expressed as a percentage of total income before tax. Total income before tax is a broader measure of income than cash income since it includes non-cash items such as interest accumulated on pension fund income but not cashed by the recipient. In this form, the data reveal some interesting comparisons.

- In 1961, the average family had to use 37.3% of its income to provide itself with shelter, food, and clothing. In the same year, 22.1% of the family's income went to government as tax.

Table 4.6: Taxes and expenditures of the average Canadian family (percentage of total income before tax)

	Taxes	Basics*	Shelter	Food	Clothing
			Expenditures		
1961	22.1	37.3	14.9	16.6	5.7
1969	27.5	33.4	13.2	14.4	5.8
1974	30.2	30.6	12.8	12.9	4.9
1976	27.3	32.4	14.3	13.0	5.1
1981	29.5	29.2	13.9	11.5	3.9
1985	31.9	30.2	15.0	10.5	4.6
1990	31.1	27.8	14.6	9.5	3.7
1992	29.6	28.4	15.3	9.6	3.5
1994	29.8	26.9	14.5	9.2	3.2
1996	30.8	25.8	14.0	8.9	2.9
1998	31.5	25.5	14.2	8.4	3.0
2000	31.8	23.3	13.0	7.7	2.6
2002	30.9	23.9	13.2	8.0	2.7
2003	30.6	23.2	13.0	7.8	2.5

Source: Table 4.5. * Sum of Shelter, Food and Clothing

Figure 4.6: Taxes and expenditures of the average Canadian family (percentage of total income before tax)

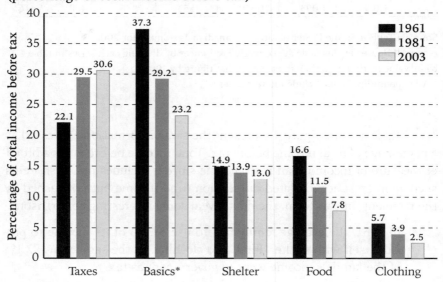

Source: Table 4.6. * Sum of shelter, food, and clothing.

- By 1981, the situation had been reversed and 29.5% of income was taken by government in the form of taxes, while only 29.2% was used to provide the family with shelter, food, and clothing.

- By 2003, the situation had become worse. Whereas the proportion of income consumed by taxes had continued to increase, the fraction of income spent on necessities (shelter, food, and clothing) had dropped dramatically. The average family spent 23.2% of its income on the necessities of life while 30.6% of its income went to taxes.

- The sum of taxes and spending on necessities accounts for 53.8% to 62.1% of total income before tax for all the years shown, with taxes representing a much larger share in 2003 than in 1961.

Tax Freedom Day

The CCTI is only one tool for evaluating the Canadian tax system. Another easily understood and revealing measure is the Tax Freedom Day of the average Canadian family. For the purposes of calculating Tax Freedom Day, the average Canadian family is the family whose income is the average income of all families with two or more members. Tax Freedom Day is that day of the year when the average family has done enough work to pay the total tax bill imposed on it by the federal, provincial, and municipal governments. It is calculated as the percentage of cash income the family pays in tax multiplied by 365 days to arrive at the number of days of work required to pay the total tax bill. If 50% of one's income goes to taxes, then one must work one-half the year for government, and one's Tax Freedom Day falls on July 2. In 1961, Tax Freedom Day fell on May 3. Since then, it has advanced 56 days, so that in 2003 it fell on June 28.

Chapter 5
The Relative Tax Burden

HOW MUCH DO I PAY? This is the first question that people ask about the tax system. Tax Freedom Day and the Canadian Consumer Tax Index discussed in the last chapter give a rough answer to this query. The next thing people want to know is how much are others paying? Are some paying less than others? These are more complicated questions because they call for a broad view of what the tax system does. Some in the media and many social activist groups believe these questions have a clear and simple answer: the "rich" pay no taxes and the poor are getting "shafted by the system." In this chapter, we suggest that the answers are not so simple. We look at all income groups and how their relative income and tax positions have changed between 1961 and 2003. A reasonable analysis of these numbers points to a different conclusion than that presented by groups that claim Canada's tax system needs to be more progressive than it is.

The distribution of income
In order to analyze the relative income and tax positions of Canadians, we have divided all Canadian families into three broad income groups based on income deciles. The first income decile is one of 10 groups that result from arranging families according to their total income before tax, from lowest to highest, and then selecting the 10% of families with the lowest incomes; the second decile is the next 10% of families, and so on. The lowest income group includes the families in the bottom three deciles;

the middle group includes the next four deciles; the upper group includes the top three deciles. The resulting groups are presented in table 5.1 and illustrated in figure 5.1.

Table 5.1 reveals that the relative shares of the different income groups have been remarkably constant over the period from 1961 through 2003. A note of caution: in evaluating this result, the reader should bear in mind that a number of aspects of the data make them susceptible to misinterpretation. First, the data fail to make any allowance for the age of individuals. This is important, since age is a principal determinant of income. Young people first entering the labour market typically earn wages or salaries considerably below the average and considerably below what will be their own lifetime average. Similarly, those who have passed the age of retirement are typically in a phase of their life when their incomes are considerably below their lifetime average and when they are spending the savings and pensions accumulated from their working lifetimes.

To illustrate this point, table 5.2 displays the "life-cycle average expected wage" for a Canadian male in 2000. Three sources of data on the earnings profile are available: information from *Income Statistics* published by Canada Customs and Revenue Agency (CCRA), Statistics Canada's income surveys, and Statistics Canada's Social Policy Simulation Database and Model (SPSD/M). While the three sources yield different estimates,

Table 5.1: Decile distribution of income before tax (%)

| | Income Groups | | |
	Lower 3 deciles (%)	Middle 4 deciles (%)	Upper 3 deciles (%)
1961	10.8	35.6	53.6
1972	9.0	33.1	57.9
1976	8.8	31.7	59.5
1981	10.0	34.9	55.0
1985	10.2	35.1	54.7
1990	8.7	33.9	57.4
1992	7.6	31.7	60.7
1994	7.9	31.9	60.3
1996	7.9	31.9	60.1
1998	8.1	32.3	59.5
2000	8.1	32.1	59.8
2002	8.1	32.2	59.7
2003	8.1	32.9	59.0

Source: The Fraser Institute's Canadian Tax Simulator 2003.

Figure 5.1: Percent of total income before tax earned by income group, 1961–2003

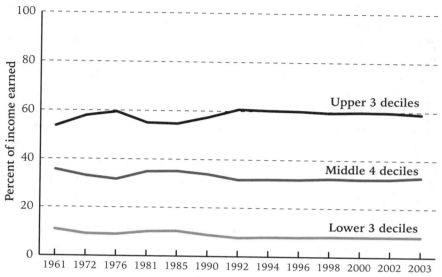

Source: The Fraser Institute's Canadian Tax Simulator 2003.

Table 5.2: Income in age groups as a percentage of average for all age groups, Canadian males, 2000

Age	CCRA income statistics (%)	Statistics Canada income survey data (%)	SPSD/M (%)	Mixed profile (%)
Under 25	32.8	32.6	31.7	32.4
25-34	87.0	96.9	94.0	92.6
35-44	121.0	126.3	126.1	124.5
45-54	135.4	134.7	138.8	136.3
55-64	121.2	111.4	112.4	115.0
65 & over	84.4	76.6	75.8	78.9

Sources: Statistics Canada, Income Trends in Canada 1980-2000, catalogue no. 13F0022; Canada Customs and Revenue Agency (CCRA), *Income Statistics*, 2002 edition (2000 Tax Year); Social Policy Simulation Database and Model (SPSD/M) (version 9.1); calculations by the authors.

they all show the large fluctuations in income relative to the average that one is likely to experience throughout one's life.

Failure to account for the age of income earners can lead to a considerably distorted impression of how income distribution is changing because there have been dramatic changes in the age structure of the population in Canada. Birth rates have declined and mortality rates have decreased since the 1960s (World Bank 2002). In 1966, the ratio of Canadians under 20 to Canadians over 65 was 5.5 to 1. This ratio decreased to 2.0 by 2001, and is projected to decline further to 1.1 by the year 2021 and to 0.94 by the year 2026 (see Statistics Canada 2002). In future years, as the number of people retired or nearing retirement grows, we can expect that the distribution of income will be affected. More of the population will be elderly and more of the population will have lower incomes as a result. This will not mean, however, that the population is, in a real sense, worse off.

A second important warning for those who would draw conclusions from these data about the equity of the income distribution is that they ignore income-in-kind that people receive from government. Housing, medical care, education, and other services that are received as direct benefits from government rather than as cash payments are not reflected in the income distribution. The public provision of these services represents one of the most substantial redistributive aspects of Canadian society.

For these reasons, it would be inappropriate to infer from the data in table 5.1 that there had been no change in the effective distribution of income since 1961. The data in their present form are incapable of providing meaningful answers to that question. What the data do provide is a yardstick against which to measure the distribution of taxes. This yardstick will allow us to infer whether, for example, groups of people with low incomes bear a disproportionate share of the tax burden. It will provide an indication of the progressivity or regressivity of the Canadian tax burden. In order to arrive at these results, it is necessary to combine income results with those on tax distribution.

Tax distribution and tax rates

Our measurements of the distribution of the tax burden provide some interesting and, indeed, puzzling results. Whereas up until the mid-1970s there had been a more or less steady increase in the total tax burden borne by the upper income group, from 1976 to 1981 the share of the top group fell markedly. As table 5.3 and figure 5.2 show, in 1976, families in the top three income deciles accounted for fully 66.5% of the total tax payments.

Table 5.3: Decile distribution of taxes (%)

	Income Groups		
	Lower 3 deciles (%)	Middle 4 deciles (%)	Upper 3 deciles (%)
1961	8.7	30.6	60.9
1972	6.0	30.0	64.0
1976	6.1	27.3	66.5
1981	6.8	33.3	59.9
1985	7.1	33.6	59.4
1990	5.5	31.7	62.8
1992	3.9	28.5	67.6
1994	4.0	28.9	67.1
1996	4.1	29.2	66.7
1998	4.2	29.5	66.3
2000	4.4	29.7	65.9
2002	4.3	29.9	65.8
2003	4.3	30.1	65.6

Source: The Fraser Institute's Canadian Tax Simulator 2003.

Figure 5.2: Percent of total taxes paid by income group, 1961–2003

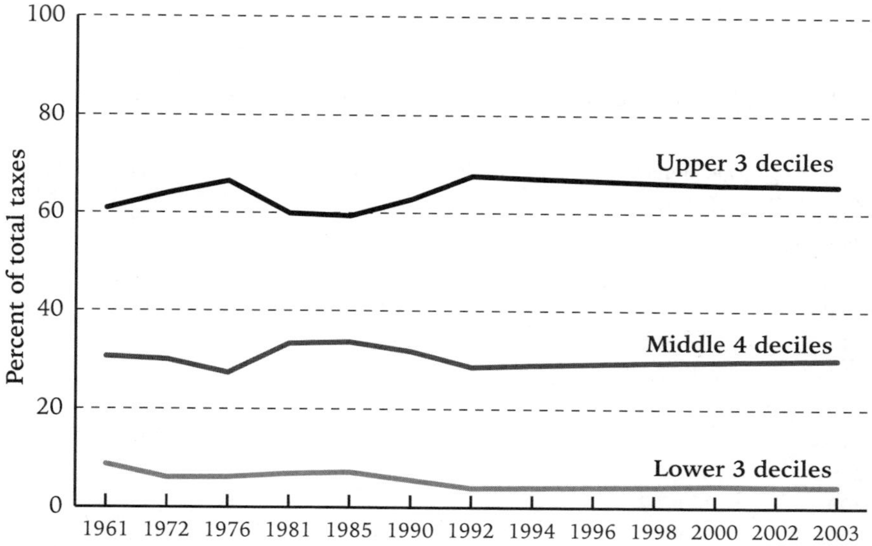

Source: The Fraser Institute's Canadian Tax Simulator 2003.

By 1981, this had fallen to 59.9% of the total, a decrease of 6.6 percentage points. The decline in the tax burden borne by the top three income deciles was nearly matched by a corresponding increase in the tax burden faced by those in the middle income deciles during this period. For example, families in the fourth to seventh income deciles, which had borne 27.3% of the total tax burden in 1976, were bearing 33.3% by 1981, an increase of 6.0 percentage points. Between 1981 and 1992, the share of the total tax burden paid by the top income group increased by 7.7 percentage points from 59.9% to 67.6% while the share paid by the middle four deciles decreased by 4.8 percentage points (33.3% to 28.5%). The trend reversed again from 1992 to 2003; during this period the total tax burden of the top 30% of income earners fell by 2.1 percentage points while the burden of the middle income group increased 1.6 percentage points.

The income tax paid by the upper income group (top three deciles) has increased significantly since 1985 while that paid by the lower two income groups (middle four and bottom three deciles) has been decreased. As table 5.4 shows, there had been a modest shift in the incidence of the personal income tax system away from the upper income deciles and toward the lower income deciles until the early and mid-1980s. This was reversed in the late 1980s and early 1990s. The top three income groups accounted for 62.7% of total income tax payments in 1981, down from 68.1% in 1976. By 2003, the top three income deciles accounted for 72.5% of total income tax payments.

Table 5.4: Decile distribution (%) of personal income taxes

| | Income Groups | | |
	Lower 3 deciles (%)	Middle 4 deciles (%)	Upper 3 deciles (%)
1976	3.2	29.5	68.1
1981	4.4	32.9	62.7
1985	4.5	34.3	61.2
1990	3.8	31.0	65.2
1992	2.1	24.7	73.1
1994	2.3	24.9	72.9
1996	2.3	25.0	72.7
1998	2.3	25.0	72.7
2000	2.3	25.3	72.4
2002	2.2	24.9	72.9
2003	2.1	25.4	72.5

Source: The Fraser Institute's Canadian Tax Simulator 2003.

A major factor explaining variations in the share of taxes paid by the top three deciles has been the change in the incidence of capital-related taxes. These are chiefly property taxes and taxes on corporate profits. As table 5.5 reveals, there have been relatively large fluctuations in the pattern of these capital-related taxes. Between 1976 and 1981, the burden of taxes on profits for the top three deciles dropped from 72.2% to 66.9%. The burden crept up to 71.8% in 1985, then fell every year until it reached 62.6% in 1998, before increasing to 63.4% in 1999. From 1999 to 2003, the share of taxes on profits paid by the top income group decreased to 61.7%.

Analysis of the underlying factors reveals that part of the reason for the dramatic shift in the incidence of capital taxes has been the change in the distribution of capital income amongst Canadians (see table 5.6). Changes in exemptions are another probable reason why capital taxes fell for the upper income deciles in the late 1970s and early 1980s, then rose in the late 1980s. For example, in the early 1980s Canadians took advantage of the tax preferences that the government inserted in the tax system to encourage the development of various sectors of the economy, such as oil exploration, rental housing, and Canadian films. The tax reform of 1987 effectively put an end to much of the tax preference game.

One factor that underlies all of the distribution series is the massive surge in the number of families in the upper income classes. In 1980, for example, only 26.1% of families had an income of $35,000 or more. By 2000, 75.8% of families enjoyed an income at least as large as that. While inflation has played a large role in this development, some of the increase in the number of families in the higher income groups is the result of the fact that an increasing number of families contain two income earners whose joint income pushes the family into the higher tax bracket.

The implication of this increase in the number of families with two income earners for the distribution of taxation amongst families is that the upper income deciles seem to be paying less and less tax because they are composed increasingly of individuals with lower incomes. As noted in chapter 2, two incomes totalling, say, $30,000 are taxed less in total than one income of $30,000. Since upper income families are increasingly composed of two income earners, this has put downward pressure on the average tax rate in this income range.

Consequently, from 1976 until 1985 the percentage of total income earned by the upper income groups had been steadily decreasing while the middle and lower income groups gained ground. This is quite clearly reflected in table 5.1, which shows the distribution of income by decile.

Table 5.5: Decile distribution (%) of profit and property taxes

Decile distribution of profit taxes

| | Income Groups | | |
	Lower 3 deciles (%)	Middle 4 deciles (%)	Upper 3 deciles (%)
1976	10.3	17.8	72.2
1981	9.1	24.0	66.9
1985	6.7	21.6	71.8
1990	5.8	24.5	69.7
1992	5.8	28.0	66.2
1994	5.5	28.6	65.9
1996	5.8	29.2	65.0
1998	6.4	31.0	62.6
2000	6.5	30.0	63.4
2002	6.5	30.9	62.6
2003	6.9	31.4	61.7

Decile distribution of property taxes

| | Income Groups | | |
	Lower 3 deciles (%)	Middle 4 deciles (%)	Upper 3 deciles (%)
1976	10.3	17.8	72.2
1981	10.9	26.8	62.3
1985	6.6	21.6	71.8
1990	5.7	24.4	69.9
1992	5.6	27.5	66.8
1994	5.5	28.4	66.1
1996	5.8	29.0	65.3
1998	6.3	31.0	62.7
2000	6.5	30.0	63.5
2002	6.5	30.9	62.5
2003	6.9	31.2	61.9

Source: The Fraser Institute's Canadian Tax Simulator 2003.

Whereas in 1976 nearly 60% of all income was earned by those in the top three deciles, this had dropped to 54.7% by 1985. After rebounding to 60.7% in 1992, the income earned by the top three deciles has steadily declined, reaching 59.0% in 2003. One further implication of the distribution of total taxes is interesting to note: figure 5.2 shows that the decline in progressivity in the tax system that began to emerge in the late 1970s was reversed by 1985.

Table 5.6: Decile distribution (%) of capital income

	Income Groups		
	Lower 3 deciles (%)	Middle 4 deciles (%)	Upper 3 deciles (%)
1976	10.3	17.8	72.2
1981	9.1	23.9	66.9
1985	6.8	22.0	71.2
1990	5.9	24.9	69.3
1992	5.8	27.9	66.3
1994	5.6	28.7	65.7
1996	5.8	29.3	64.9
1998	6.4	31.2	62.4
2000	6.6	30.2	63.2
2002	6.6	31.3	62.1
2003	7.0	31.6	61.4

Source: The Fraser Institute's Canadian Tax Simulator 2003.

A look across the generations

The tables on income distribution presented above give only a snapshot of the number of Canadians who fall into various income groups at one point in time. We must look at these tables with an understanding of what they can and cannot tell us. These tables are perfectly adequate for showing that our tax system is progressive and how much current upper income groups pay versus current lower income groups. What these tables do not show is that, while there is a fairly constant proportion of the population in these income groups, the composition of these groups changes significantly from year to year. What this means is that there is not a "permanent under-class" stuck in the lower income group.

From simulations of lifetime income and taxes done for previous editions of this book, we know that the average lifetime tax rate is higher than the average tax rate from the snapshot. We also know that there is less inequality in average lifetime tax rates than suggested by the snapshot. This should come as no surprise since many young families start out in the low income group and work up to the middle or high income group. There is less inequality in the long term because many families will initially have low income and low taxes followed by middle income and middle taxes and possibly high income and high taxes as they move through their life cycles.

Evidence of just how much the composition of income groups fluctuates has been released from Statistics Canada's Survey of Labour and Income Dynamics. Table 5.7 shows the shifts in the position of a groups of people in the overall income distribution between 1996 and 1997. This table shows that there were 3.059 million people in the third income quintile in both 1996 and 1997, that 1.022 million who were in the third quintile in 1996 had moved up to the fourth in 1997, and that 0.759 million people dropped from the third to the second quintile between 1996 and 1997. Between 1996 and 1997:

- 66.8% of families did not change quintile

- 14.2% moved up one quintile

- 12.2% dropped one quintile

- 3.1% moved up more than one quintile

- 3.8% dropped more than one quintile

Nearly one quarter (23%) of those families in the bottom two quintiles in 1996 were at least one quintile higher by 1997. Extending the study period from two to five years shows greater income mobility (Webber et al. 1999). The data show that:

Table 5.7: People classified by their family income quintile in 1996 and 1997 (thousands)

		Income quintile in 1997			
		First (bottom)	Second	Third	Fourth	Fifth (top)
Income quintile in 1996	First (bottom)	4,019	903	245	110	41
	Second	793	3,351	936	170	63
	Third	298	759	3,059	1,022	191
	Fourth	125	209	868	3,196	905
	Fifth (top)	80	92	206	816	4,114

Sources: Statistics Canada, A Comparison of the Results from the Survey of Labour and Income Dynamics (SLID) and the Survey of Consumer Finances (SCF), 1993-1997: Updated, product number 75F0002MIE-99007, 1999.

- 49.1% of families did not change quintile

- 20.7% moved up one quintile

- 14.5% dropped one quintile

- 8.2% moved up more than one quintile

- 7.5% dropped more than one quintile

Of those initially in the bottom two quintiles, 45% moved up at least one quintile over the five-year period of the study.

Who pays the tax bill?

Table 5.3 shows that the largest portion of the tax burden ultimately settles on the higher income groups. In 2003, the top 30% of families earned 59.0% of all income in Canada and paid 65.6% of all taxes. The bottom 30% earned 8.1% of all income and paid 4.3% of all taxes.

To economists these figures are nothing out of the ordinary. Our tax system is progressive. It is not surprising to find that those earning lower income pay less tax as a proportion of their income than those earning higher income. This result may, however, come as a surprise to activists and reporters who claim that the "rich" in Canada pay no taxes. As tables 5.3 and 5.4 show, the rich bear most of Canada's taxation burden. Some critics might counter that the rich in Canada avoid taxes by holding their wealth in corporations and that corporations can avoid taxes better than individuals. We address this question in chapter 7 and present the results of a study done by the Ontario government's Fair Tax Commission, which found that corporations do pay their taxes.

Who belongs to the club of the top 30% of Canadian families? A Canadian family is included in the top 30% when its cash income exceeds $73,016. The average income in this group is $122,882.

Get it from the rich

It is often said—and all too often believed—that the key to "social welfare" or "social justice" is the redistribution of income. That is, the state should take income from those who have more and give it to those who have less. The extreme form of this prescription is "from each according to his ability [to pay] and to each according to his need"—the rule advanced in the Communist Manifesto (Marx and Engels 1848).

The preceding section's analysis of who pays the income tax reveals that, as a country, Canada already engages in significant taxation of those who are relatively well-off. It remains interesting, therefore, to inquire whether or not we could achieve a more equal distribution of the benefits of the Canadian good life by taxing more of the income of the richest Canadians.

How rich is rich?

The question that immediately arises is "How rich is rich?" At what income level should the government tax away all increases in the interest of "equitable" income distribution? Many of the top provincial statutory income tax rates apply at or around $60,000. Let us, then, for the sake of illustration, select $60,000 as the maximum income that Canadians should be allowed to earn. Under this rule, all incomes above $60,000 would be subject to a 100% rate of income tax and the proceeds would be distributed to all income earners with incomes less than $60,000.

Counting the rich

In 2001, 2,434,190 persons filed tax returns reporting an income of $60,000 or more. Note that, in this section, individual and not family incomes, are the focus of the analysis. Note also that this section examines personal income tax, not the total tax burden. Total income reported by these people was $260 billion. If the government had really taxed away all income beyond $60,000, the total tax revenue in 2001 would have been $50.7 billion higher than it actually was. Redistribution of this increased tax revenue to those 19.2 million tax filers with incomes less than $60,000 would yield an average annual payment of $2,649.

Taxing the "rich" is not
the source of wealth

This calculation is important because it reveals the practical impossibility of "getting it from the rich and redistributing it to the poor." A look back to table 2.6 reveals that only 11.3% of tax filers earned more than $60,000 in 2001. Those who are impatient with the speed at which the economic process improves the condition of the poorest members of society ought to reflect on the fact that the same total increase in the incomes of those earning less than $60,000 would be achieved by about a 5.8% growth in total incomes, even if it were distributed in exactly the same way as it is now. What Canada needs are more "rich" people; imposing more taxes is not the way to increase anyone's wealth.

The rags-to-riches tax burden

In the previous sections, we have shown in general terms how our progressive tax system imposes ever increasing burdens on people as they earn more income. What about an individual who started off in 1961 with meagre earnings and has since improved his economic situation markedly? What kind of message does our tax system send to this person? Table 5.8 presents the results of a tax analysis for such an individual. We assume that when he started working in 1961 he was earning $2,750 a year in cash income, half the average income, and that his income grew steadily and at such a rate that by 2003 he was earning twice the average, or $116,513 a year.

In 1961, this person's total income before tax of $4,775 attracted a tax bill of $960 or an average tax rate on total income of 20.1%. By 1973, the hypothetical income earner had a total income before tax of $13,371 and paid taxes of $3,145, for a tax rate of 23.5%. Finally, in 2003, when his cash income was $116,513, his total income before tax was $175,456, and his taxes paid amounted to $61,083. Thus, the average tax rate on total income before tax had risen from 20.1% to 34.8%.

Over the period of 42 years from 1961 to 2003, our hypothetical income earner experienced a 3,574% increase in total income before tax. Over the same period, his taxes paid increased by 6,263% and taxes as a percentage of total income before tax increased by 73.2%.

Table 5.8: The rags-to-riches tax burden

	Cash income ($)	Total income before tax ($)	Tax ($)	Tax as a percentage of total income before tax
1961	2,750	4,775	960	20.1
1973	8,021	13,371	3,145	23.5
1983	19,570	31,538	8,454	26.8
1993	47,751	74,388	22,724	30.5
2003	116,513	175,456	61,083	34.8
Increase (%) 1961–2003	4,137	3,574	6,263	73.2

Source: The Fraser Institute's Canadian Tax Simulator 2003.

Marginal versus average tax rates

The tax rate that one earns on the next dollar of income is referred to as the "marginal tax rate." It can differ dramatically from the average tax rate, which is the rate that we are most accustomed to thinking about. Table 5.9 shows both marginal and average rates for different income levels; figure 5.3 illustrates them.

It is this marginal rate that enters into people's decisions about how much to work. When someone decides whether or not to work an extra hour, she asks herself how much extra she will earn and how much extra tax she will pay. She does not consider how much tax on average she is paying because this does not reflect the true return to any extra effort she may wish to provide. As table 5.9 shows, these rates jump considerably as one moves from the second to the third income decile, reflecting that initially it is very costly to work because one rapidly loses social assistance. The reason for this result is that many social assistance payments are reduced (the gains are "clawed back") once the recipient starts earning income. In effect, these "claw-backs" can cause the tax rate on the first few dollars of earned income to be very high. This effect fades in the middle income brackets but rises again at higher levels of income from the effect of increasing progressivity.

Figure 5.3: Average and marginal tax rates by income decile, 2003

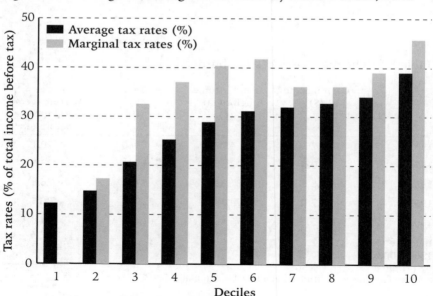

Source: The Fraser Institute's Canadian Tax Simulator 2003.

Table 5.9: Average and marginal tax rates (%) in Canada, 2003

Average tax rates (%)

Lower income groups			Middle income groups				Upper income groups		
1	2	3	4	5	6	7	8	9	10
Income measure = cash income									
15.3	19.1	29.1	37.7	44.8	47.2	48.1	49.5	51.3	59.1
Income measure = total income before tax									
12.0	14.7	20.6	25.2	28.8	31.1	31.9	32.7	34.0	39.0

Marginal tax rates (%) faced when moving from a lower to a higher decile

1 to 2	2 to 3	3 to 4	4 to 5	5 to 6	6 to 7	7 to 8	8 to 9	9 to 10
Income measure = cash income								
22.6	55.9	65.3	72.2	57.0	52.1	56.3	58.0	69.5
Income measure = total income before tax								
17.2	32.5	37.0	40.3	41.7	36.1	36.1	39.0	45.6

Source: The Fraser Institute's Canadian Tax Simulator 2003.

Chapter 6
Taxes across Canada

Taxes are the price one pays for government services. If taxes were the same in all provinces, the first five chapters of this book would be a sufficient price guide to government services. As taxes differ from province to province, however, we need to break our analysis down by province. This breakdown may be of interest to Canadians who want an idea of where taxes are lightest and where they are heaviest. It may also be of interest to government officials who understand that it is dangerous for the economic health of a province when it imposes significantly more tax than its neighbours. Figure 6.1 shows the tax rate as a percent of cash income for the average Canadian family by province.

In comparing the provinces, we must make some adjustment for the fact that family size differs from province to province. The family whose income is average in Newfoundland and Labrador has more members than its counterpart in Ontario. Put differently, Newfoundland and Labrador has relatively fewer single-member families than does Ontario. We would not be comparing the same sort of family if we set these averages side by side. To get a more precise comparison, this chapter focuses on families of two or more individuals. However, the appendix shows that many of the results hold for families and unattached individuals, and families of two parents with two children under the age of 18.

Table 6.1 (pages 70–71) presents the tax situation for the average family by province of residence. In this context, "average family" means a family unit that has an average income in its province of residence. Thus,

Figure 6.1: Tax rates of the average family, 2003

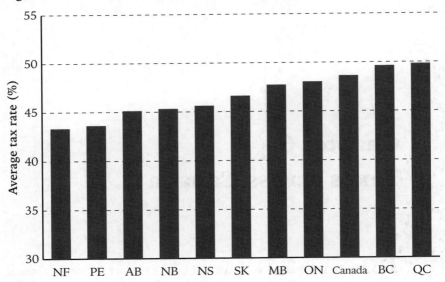

Source: The Fraser Institute's Canadian Tax Simulator 2003.

for example, the average family in Newfoundland and Labrador had a cash income of $57,111 in 2003 whereas the average family in Ontario had an income of $81,437 in the same year, and so on. Table 6.2 shows which provinces have the highest propensity to tax in each of the tax categories. Income tax makes up between 28.0% and 37.4% of the family's tax bill. The highest rate is in Alberta, where the average family provides 37.4% of its taxes in income tax. The lowest proportion is in Saskatchewan, at 28.0%. The Maritimes rely most heavily upon the sales tax. For instance, 21.4¢ out of each dollar paid in taxes by the average family in Prince Edward Island are collected as sales tax. By comparison, 15.9¢ and 16.7¢ out of each tax dollar are collected as sales tax from the average Saskatchewan and British Columbian family, while just 8.4¢ per tax dollar are collected from that source from the average Albertan family, as Alberta has no provincial sales tax. Saskatchewan has the highest reliance on property tax, collecting 8.7% of taxes in this form, whereas Newfoundland only collects 4.2% of its taxes as property tax.

Saskatchewan, Alberta, and British Columbia are the only provinces that have significant natural-resource revenues. In Alberta, for example, petroleum-related taxes are not collected from the tax-paying public; rather, they are collected from the corporations that remove oil and gas from the ground. It is nevertheless the case that the oil and gas in the ground in Alberta belongs to the people of Alberta. Since they do not receive the income from these natural resources, it is appropriate to regard the taxes that are paid as a result of exploitation of these petroleum resources as a tax on Albertans.

While this is the appropriate technical treatment of petroleum resource taxes, apportioning these taxes in this way does confuse somewhat the inter-provincial comparison of tax burdens. If we subtracted from the $39,565 total tax bill faced by the average Albertan family the $2,211 collected on their behalf from the petroleum industry, we find that the total tax bill is reduced to $37,354 for the average family. Without natural-resource taxes, the tax bill for Saskatchewan and British Columbia would be $27,012 and $31,970, respectively. Table 6.3 presents the ratios of taxes to income for the average family with, and without, natural-resource levies for the provinces that have significant revenues from this tax source.

In comparing the tax results for the various provinces, it is important to remember that the standard of comparison is the average family, the family in each province whose income is average. Since the average income in each province varies considerably, some of the differences in the tax burden among the provinces is due to nothing more than differences in income.

Table 6.4 provides a distribution of taxes by province according to income deciles. The great benefit of this table is that it makes possible a comparison of how the tax burden is distributed amongst the various income groups within each province. The outcome of this analysis, as reflected in the table, is remarkable; there is little variation among the provinces in the extent of the progressivity or regressivity of their various tax systems. The upper income groups in all provinces absorb between 61.9% and 67.9% of the total tax bill.

The similarity of the tax distributions in the provinces is note-worthy because it exists in spite of the differences in the provincial tax systems. These differences, which were pointed out above in the discussion of tables 6.1 and 6.2, ought to provide some variation in the tax rates unless, as is apparent from table 6.4, the differences in the progressivity and regressivity of the various taxes largely offset one other.

There are, however, some important differences between the tax systems in the various provinces. Table 6.5 highlights the differences in

Table 6.1: Taxes of the average Canadian family (two or more

	Average cash income	Average total income before tax	Income tax	Sales tax	Amusement taxes*	Automobile taxes**
NF	57,111	89,010	8,034	4,933	2,217	1,043
PEI	59,788	91,430	8,215	5,575	2,079	988
NS	60,934	94,011	9,400	4,973	2,210	992
NB	60,812	93,044	8644	5,055	1,957	1,217
QC	66,558	101,242	11,639	6,079	2,016	927
ON	81,437	124,610	13,254	6,931	2,321	1,001
MB	69,622	105,707	11,165	5,604	2,557	880
SK	60,348	95,601	7,862	4,474	2,073	1,290
AB	87,686	135,860	14,785	3,326	3,282	855
BC	66,816	104,315	9,940	5,550	2,275	857
Canada	73,718	113,612	12,081	6,031	2,342	986

Source: The Fraser Institute's Canadian Tax Simulator 2003. * Amusement taxes include bile, fuel, and motor vehicle license taxes; *** payroll taxes include social security, pension,

Table 6.2: Individual taxes as a proportion of the total tax bill

	Income tax	Sales tax	Amusement taxes*	Automobile taxes**
NF	32.5	20.0	9.0	4.2
PEI	31.5	21.4	8.0	3.8
NS	33.8	17.9	8.0	3.6
NB	31.3	18.3	7.1	4.4
QC	35.1	18.3	6.1	2.8
ON	33.9	17.7	5.9	2.6
MB	33.6	16.9	7.7	2.7
SK	28.0	15.9	7.4	4.6
AB	37.4	8.4	8.3	2.2
BC	30.0	16.7	6.9	2.6
Canada	33.7	16.8	6.5	2.8

Source: The Fraser Institute's Canadian Tax Simulator 2003. *Amusement taxes include bile, fuel, and motor vehicle license taxes; *** payroll taxes include social security, pension,

individuals), 2003 (dollars)

Payroll taxes***	Property tax	Import duties	Profits tax	Natural resource taxes	Other taxes	Total taxes
4,621	1,039	189	1,360	376	909	24,720
5,075	1,582	221	1,827	9	473	26,043
4,903	2,167	235	2,619	50	253	27,802
5,671	2,209	247	1,962	124	490	27,574
7,922	1,804	276	2,068	25	373	33,131
8,142	3,120	357	3,160	28	757	39,071
5,923	2,239	298	2,787	71	1,658	33,183
4,809	2,458	238	3,098	1,116	710	28,128
7,729	2,707	368	3,075	2,211	1,227	39,565
7,037	2,456	303	2,549	1,188	1,003	33,157
7,544	2,569	316	2,763	423	753	35,808

liquor, tobacco, amusement, and other excise taxes; ** automobile taxes include automo-
medical, and hospital taxes.

for the average family (two or more individuals), 2003 (%)

Payroll taxes***	Property tax	Import duties	Profits tax	Natural resource taxes	Other taxes
18.7	4.2	0.8	5.5	1.5	3.7
19.5	6.1	0.8	7.0	0.0	1.8
17.6	7.8	0.8	9.4	0.2	0.9
20.6	8.0	0.9	7.1	0.4	1.8
23.9	5.4	0.8	6.2	0.1	1.1
20.8	8.0	0.9	8.1	0.1	1.9
17.9	6.7	0.9	8.4	0.2	5.0
17.1	8.7	0.8	11.0	4.0	2.5
19.5	6.8	0.9	7.8	5.6	3.1
21.2	7.4	0.9	7.7	3.6	3.0
21.1	7.2	0.9	7.7	1.2	2.1

liquor, tobacco, amusement, and other excise taxes; ** automobile taxes include automo-
medical, and hospital taxes.

Table 6.3: Ratios of taxes to cash income and to total income before taxes for an average family (two or more individuals), 2003

	Ratio (%) of taxes to cash income	Ratio (%) of taxes to total income before tax
Newfoundland and Labrador	43.3	27.8
Prince Edward Island	43.6	28.5
Nova Scotia	45.6	29.6
New Brunswick	45.3	29.6
Quebec	49.8	32.7
Ontario	48.0	31.4
Manitoba	47.7	31.4
Saskatchewan	46.6	29.4
Alberta	45.1	29.1
British Columbia	49.6	31.8
Canada	48.6	31.5
Ratio (%) excluding natural resources taxes		
Saskatchewan	44.8	28.3
Alberta	42.6	27.5
British Columbia	47.8	30.6
Canada	48.0	31.1

Source: The Fraser Institute's Canadian Tax Simulator 2003.

Table 6.4: Decile distribution of taxes (%), by province, 2003

	Lower 3 deciles (%)	Middle 4 deciles (%)	Upper 3 deciles (%)
Newfoundland and Labrador	1.9	30.2	67.9
Prince Edward Island	4.1	31.9	64.0
Nova Scotia	5.2	32.9	61.9
New Brunswick	2.3	29.9	67.8
Quebec	4.7	31.1	64.2
Ontario	4.9	29.2	65.9
Manitoba	3.8	32.7	63.5
Saskatchewan	5.7	30.8	63.4
Alberta	4.5	30.5	64.9
British Columbia	3.0	29.2	67.8
Canada	4.3	30.1	65.6

Source: The Fraser Institute's Canadian Tax Simulator 2003.

average tax rates payable by the various income deciles in each province. Thus, in Prince Edward Island for example, the lowest income decile paid a tax rate of 4.2% on average whereas the top decile paid a tax rate of 36.7%. In Saskatchewan, on the other hand, the bottom decile paid 14.7% while the top decile paid 37.8%.

Underlying this pattern of taxation is a pattern of government expenditures: the reason for raising revenues is to pay for government spending. Accordingly, an alternative, and perhaps more direct, measure of the level of government activity is the level of government spending. Table 6.6 presents both the total amounts and the per-capita amounts of provincial government spending in each of the provinces, adjusted for the amount of that spending that is financed by federal transfers to each province.

Table 6.6 reveals an interesting pattern of spending, especially when compared with the taxation data. The data reveal that Quebec and British Columbia are among the provinces that spend the most and tax the most while the Maritime provinces, when transfer payments are removed, are among those that spend the least and tax the least.

Table 6.5: Average tax rates on total income before tax by decile and province, 2003 (%)

	Lower income groups			Middle income groups				Upper income groups		
	1	2	3	4	5	6	7	8	9	10
NF	7.1	4.7	10.7	19.8	24.0	26.4	30.4	32.0	32.5	31.2
PEI	4.2	12.0	17.6	23.0	24.4	27.4	30.8	30.4	33.5	36.7
NS	10.9	16.4	19.3	23.7	28.5	30.9	31.6	31.5	32.9	36.0
NB	6.3	4.7	13.6	20.0	25.3	28.1	30.7	32.2	33.5	37.2
QC	12.1	16.7	21.0	24.9	30.3	33.6	33.6	35.1	36.6	41.4
ON	12.5	17.6	23.1	26.3	29.2	30.8	31.5	32.5	33.4	40.5
MB	9.0	10.1	17.5	22.8	29.1	31.4	31.7	33.2	34.5	38.0
SK	14.7	15.7	19.6	22.8	26.8	29.5	30.9	31.7	33.1	37.8
AB	13.1	12.3	20.0	24.7	26.9	26.9	29.0	30.5	31.3	34.6
BC	10.7	12.3	16.8	23.3	27.4	30.4	32.3	32.8	32.8	38.8
Canada	12.0	14.7	20.6	25.2	28.8	31.1	31.9	32.7	34.0	39.0

Source: The Fraser Institute's Canadian Tax Simulator 2003.

Table 6.6: Provincial government spending, 2003/04

	Total Spending ($ millions)	Amounts per person			Rank by spending (net of transfers)	Rank by taxation
		Total Spending ($)	Federal transfers ($)	Spending net of transfers ($)		
NF	3,916	7,421	2,841	4,580	8	10
PEI	1,052	7,481	2,874	4,608	7	9
NS	5,636	5,951	2,087	3,864	10	6
NB	5,475	7,226	2,494	4,733	6	7
QC	*51,864	6,928	1,280	5,648	3	1
ON	70,566	5,766	832	4,934	5	3
MB	7,256	6,289	2,174	4,115	9	4
SK	6,621	6,555	1,044	5,511	4	5
AB	20,800	6,556	752	5,804	1	8
BC	27,800	6,654	955	5,698	2	2

Sources: Provincial budgets; Statistics Canada, Provincial Economic Accounts; The Fraser Institute's Canadian Tax Simulator 2003; calculations by authors. * Total provincial spending by Quebec is adjusted for abatements.

Appendix

This appendix presents the tax calculations for two other family types:

- families and unattached individuals (the focus of chapters 3, 4, and 5)—tables 6.7 (page 75) and 6.8 (pages 76–77), and

- families of four consisting of two parents and two children under the age of 18—tables 6.9 (page 75) and 6.10 (pages 76–77).

Table 6.7: Ratios (%) of taxes to cash income and to total income before taxes for families and unattached individuals, 2003

	Ratio (%) of taxes to cash income	Ratio (%) of taxes to total income before tax
Newfoundland	42.7	27.3
Prince Edward Island	42.0	27.6
Nova Scotia	45.2	29.3
New Brunswick	43.5	28.5
Quebec	48.4	31.8
Ontario	47.2	30.8
Manitoba	46.3	30.5
Saskatchewan	45.0	28.7
Alberta	44.3	28.4
British Columbia	48.9	31.2
Canada	47.0	30.6

Source: The Fraser Institute's Canadian Tax Simulator 2003.

Table 6.9: Ratios (%) of taxes to cash income and to total income before taxes for families of four (parents and two children under 18), 2003

	Ratio (%) of taxes to cash income	Ratio (%) of taxes to total income before tax
Newfoundland	45.4	29.1
Prince Edward Island	43.3	28.2
Nova Scotia	46.5	30.3
New Brunswick	45.1	29.9
Quebec	50.7	34.1
Ontario	45.0	30.7
Manitoba	46.7	31.4
Saskatchewan	48.0	30.5
Alberta	42.2	28.9
British Columbia	48.3	32.0
Canada	46.8	31.5

Source: The Fraser Institute's Canadian Tax Simulator 2003.

Table 6.8: Taxes of families and unattached individuals, 2003 (dollars)

	Average cash income	Average total income before tax	Income tax	Sales tax	Amusement taxes*	Automobile taxes**
NF	48,229	75,447	6,403	3,998	1,797	845
PE	49,596	75,440	6,338	4,396	1,639	779
NS	49,741	76,715	7,375	3,908	1,737	779
NB	49,924	76,171	6,239	3,849	1,490	926
QC	52,387	79,874	8,411	4,489	1,489	684
ON	65,745	100,745	10,056	5,427	1,817	784
MB	57,453	87,156	8,506	4,320	1,971	678
SK	48,908	76,637	6,001	3,356	1,555	968
AB	69,905	109,232	10,926	2,587	2,552	665
BC	50,914	79,731	7,014	4,019	1,648	620
Canada	58,782	90,458	8,887	4,507	1,772	733

Source: The Fraser Institute's Canadian Tax Simulator 2003. *Amusement taxes include bile, fuel, and motor vehicle license taxes; *** payroll taxes include social security, pension,

Table 6.10: Taxes of families of four (parents and two children under 18),

	Average cash income	Average total income before tax	Income tax	Sales tax	Amusement taxes*	Automobile taxes**
NF	64,555	100,749	10,404	6,092	2,738	1,288
PE	61,876	95,073	8,982	6,144	2,291	1,089
NS	71,269	109,347	12,798	6,545	2,909	1,305
NB	68,105	102,692	11,159	6,185	2,395	1,489
QC	81,057	120,517	16,426	8,014	2,658	1,222
ON	89,100	130,549	15,628	8,003	2,679	1,156
MB	73,977	110,002	12,956	6,536	2,982	1,026
SK	76,544	120,517	12,394	6,445	2,986	1,858
AB	95,349	139,349	16,843	3,716	3,667	956
BC	81,915	123,692	13,914	7,170	2,939	1,107
Canada	84,318	125,350	15,273	7,250	2,849	1,185

Source: The Fraser Institute's Canadian Tax Simulator 2003. *Amusement taxes include bile, fuel, and motor vehicle license taxes. *** payroll taxes include social security, pension,

Payroll taxes***	Property tax	Import duties	Profits tax	Natural resource taxes	Other taxes	Total taxes
3,640	1,173	153	1,535	289	741	20,574
3,894	1,491	174	1,723	7	378	20,820
3,815	2,015	185	2,434	38	199	22,485
4,278	2,260	188	2,008	100	381	21,719
5,751	1,886	204	2,161	18	276	25,369
6,373	2,826	280	2,862	23	592	31,038
4,468	2,277	230	2,835	56	1,283	26,623
3,497	2,260	178	2,849	809	533	22,006
6,145	2,401	286	2,727	1,748	956	30,994
5,007	2,338	219	2,426	855	732	24,878
5,659	2,375	241	2,556	333	578	27,640

liquor, tobacco, amusement, and other excise taxes; ** automobile taxes include automo-
medical, and hospital taxes.

2003 (dollars)

Payroll taxes***	Property tax	Import duties	Profits tax	Natural resource taxes	Other taxes	Total taxes
6,130	344	233	450	526	1,108	29,314
6,147	646	244	746	12	513	26,813
6,856	905	309	1,093	70	333	33,123
7,260	626	302	556	169	586	30,727
10,672	552	364	632	36	492	41,068
9,853	734	413	743	36	874	40,117
7,436	543	348	675	96	1,925	34,522
7,542	1,173	342	1,479	1,529	1,023	36,772
8,613	919	411	1,044	2,687	1,365	40,219
9,449	869	391	901	1,577	1,284	39,602
9,486	743	384	808	580	916	39,475

liquor, tobacco, amusement, and other excise taxes; ** automobile taxes include automo-
medical, and hospital taxes.

Chapter 7
Who Pays the Corporate Tax?

CORPORATIONS ARE A MAJOR SOURCE OF REVENUE for federal and provincial governments. In 2002, they paid $40.4 billion in direct taxes, 10.3% of all federal and provincial government takings (tables 7.1 and 7.5). These statements are factually correct but misleading. "Corporations" do not really bear the burden of these taxes—people do. This chapter explains which people end up paying these taxes. Even though we are well furnished with data on how much corporations pay and who owns them, determining who pays the corporate tax is not straightforward. A tax on corporations is a tax on capital. When the tax rises, capital will flee and this will affect what capital and labour earn and what consumers pay. Who truly ends up bearing the tax depends on all these effects. Our calculations suggest that the elderly bear the brunt of corporate taxation.

Background on corporations and corporate tax

A corporation is a group of people bound by contract to work together and to share the rewards of that work; in its simplest terms, it is a joint venture between capitalists and workers. This description is too rudimentary to be of much help in explaining why corporations exist and to what subtle incentives they respond but it is all we need for the present discussion. Profit is what is left after labour, interest on capital, and the cost of materials have been paid, and this residual amount can be thought of as going to the people who provided the capital for the business. Corporate tax falls on profits. This is why the corporate tax is a tax on capital.

There is often confusion over what the corporate tax rate is because, as well as having their profits taxed, corporations may receive special tax breaks that allow them to write off more than their true capital expenses. This means a corporation may pay a high statutory rate on its profits but a much lower actual rate because of its deductions.

Statutory rates on capital rose in the 1970s and 1980s but revenue from the corporate tax was unsteady because profits varied and deductions had increased, eroding the tax base. It is a general principle of taxation that, if a government wants to raise a certain amount of revenue, it will distort people's choices less by imposing a low tax on a broad base than a high tax on a narrow base. By the mid-1980s, the base had become too narrow and this prompted the first stage of corporate tax reform. In the 1986 budget, the federal government started phasing out deductions such as the inventory allowance and the investment-tax credit and announced a leisurely pace at which it would reduce the statutory tax rate by 3% on average. However, tax reform in the United States lowered the corporate rate by 12% and this forced Canada to accelerate its own reforms, fearing that it would lose tax revenue to the United States because multinationals would report their revenue in the United States and their costs in Canada.

In 1987, many exemptions in the Canadian system were reduced and tax rates were decreased to 28% for large non-manufacturing firms, 23% for large manufacturing firms, and 12% for small firms. In 2002, the rates were 25% for large non-manufacturing firms, 21% for large manufacturing firms, and 12% for small firms. The 25% rate for large non-manufacturing firms is scheduled to decline from 23% in 2003 to 21% in 2004. All provinces also levy corporate income tax, though at lower rates. Table 7.1 and the accompanying figure 7.1 show how federal and provincial corporate tax revenues have varied between 1961 and 2002.

Why is the corporate tax so popular?

The corporate tax has great political appeal. Ministers of finance argue convincingly that if a corporation makes profits it should pay taxes just as ordinary working people do. This argument is appealing but hides from Canadians the fact that, in the end, ordinary Canadians pay the corporate income tax. We can see this by asking what a corporation is: it is composed of machinery, contracts, office space, employees, shareholders, bondholders, and so on. These parts work together to make income for people and corporate tax is, therefore, a tax on people. The corporation itself cannot pay the tax because it is not the final destination of the

Table 7.1: Corporate tax collections, 1961 to 2002 ($millions 2002)

	Provincial	Federal	Total
1961	1,935	8,559	10,494
1963	2,969	8,751	11,720
1965	3,243	9,829	13,072
1967	3,531	9,730	13,262
1969	4,165	12,215	16,380
1971	4,153	11,838	15,991
1973	6,081	15,428	21,509
1975	7,292	18,557	25,849
1977	6,256	15,277	21,533
1979	7,945	17,150	25,095
1981	7,017	18,836	25,853
1983	4,794	16,422	21,217
1985	6,310	18,383	24,693
1987	7,485	17,323	24,807
1989	8,603	16,221	24,824
1991	6,189	11,951	18,140
1993	6,509	12,502	19,011
1995	10,011	15,271	25,282
1997	13,295	22,372	35,667
1999	14,659	27,782	42,442
2001	13,549	25,133	38,682
2002	14,601	25,749	40,350

Sources: Statistics Canada, National Economic and Financial Accounts, catalogue no. 13-001-XPB; calculations by the authors.

income it generates. On the contrary, as the next sections show, taxes imposed on the corporation fan out to the general public by a path that is hard to trace. As J.B. Colbert said in 1665, "The art of taxation consists in so plucking the goose as to obtain the largest amount of feathers with the least possible amount of hissing" (Mencken 1989: s.v. "Taxes") Corporate taxes cause less "hissing" than the more obvious taxes on sales or personal income. This is why politicians like the corporate tax.

Should it be so popular?
Who, in the end, pays the corporate tax? There are, of course, corporations owned by wealthy families and these families bear a portion of the tax. There are also many ordinary working people, however, who entrust

Figure 7.1: Corporate tax revenue, 1961–2002 ($billions 2002)

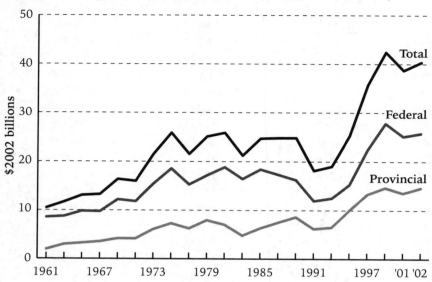

Sources: Statistics Canada, National Economic and Financial Accounts, Catalogue No. 13–001–XPB; calculations by the authors.

their savings to mutual-fund managers. These managers invest this money in corporations and the income of those corporations flows back to these small investors. In fact, every working Canadian that earns above $3500, indirectly owns shares in Canadian banks and many other corporations. This is because each person earning over $3500 must contribute to the Canadian Pension Plan (CPP) and these contributions are managed by the Canada Pension Plan Investment Board, which invests the funds received in assets such as bonds and stocks to maximize returns. In addition, money set aside by employers for pensions is also invested in corporations. For example, OMERS, the Ontario Municipal Employees' Retirement System, is one of the largest stock owners and traders in Canada.

What is less obvious, but equally true, is that home-owners, farmers, cab drivers, and anyone who owns capital in the non-corporate sector of the economy also feels the impact of taxes on the corporate sector. How can this be? The reason is that capital is highly mobile. If the opportunities for making money in the corporate sector are reduced, investors will look for opportunities abroad or in the non-corporate sector—largely agriculture and real estate—at home. As investors transfer their corporate capital to this sector, capital will become more abundant there and the returns to capital there will fall. For example, those who invest in high-technology stocks may find the corporate tax gives them too little return for the risks involved and they may decide to invest their money in apartment buildings. This will add to the number of rental apartments, increase the vacancy rate, and lower the margins of profit for landlords. Thus, the tax in the corporate high-technology sector can also affect the market for commercial real estate.

This is one of many possible examples that show why measuring who ultimately pays the corporate tax is a difficult task. There are other factors that add to the complexity of allocating the corporate tax burden: companies can pass the tax on as higher prices or capital can leave the country, thereby making labour less productive and reducing wages.

Estimating the Canadian corporate tax

Since none of these assumptions can be dismissed out of hand, there is bound to be controversy over any estimate of who bears the corporate tax. This is why we provide several sets of calculations, each based on different, but plausible, assumptions. The main assumption we use in our calculations is that owners of capital in both corporate and non-corporate sectors bear the corporate tax but, for balance, we show what some of our results would look like if labour bore the entire tax or if it were shared between capital and labour.

Table 7.2 shows the breakdown of the corporate tax by lower-income, middle-income, and upper-income groups. As expected, the upper-income group bears most of this tax. Income deciles, however, do not tell us anything about the personal characteristics of taxpayers. A crucial question is how much of the tax various age groups pay. Table 7.3 and figure 7.2 show how much of all taxes that the government collects are paid by people of different age groups and compares this to how much corporate tax each age group pays. Even though people over 65 years of age pay little in overall taxes, they bear a disproportionate amount of the corporate tax.

These results are not surprising given our assumption that capital bears the tax. The elderly and the retired receive most of their income from capital sources such as retirement funds and rental property. For comparison, figure 7.3 shows how much different age groups would pay under the assumptions that (1) capital bears the entire tax; (2) capital and labour share the burden equally (i.e., capital and labour bear the tax in proportion to their shares in national income); (3) labour bears the entire

Table 7.2: Decile distribution of profit taxes (%)

	Income Groups		
	Lower 3 deciles (%)	Middle 4 deciles (%)	Upper 3 deciles (%)
1976	10.3	17.8	72.2
1981	9.1	24.0	66.9
1985	6.7	21.6	71.8
1990	5.8	24.5	69.7
1992	5.8	28.0	66.2
1994	5.5	28.6	65.9
1996	5.8	29.2	65.0
1998	6.4	31.0	62.6
2000	6.5	30.0	63.4
2002	6.5	30.9	62.6
2003	6.9	31.4	61.7

Source: The Fraser Institute's Canadian Tax Simulator 2003.

Table 7.3: Total tax and corporate tax paid, by age group, 2003

Age group	Corporate tax ($ millions)	Share of corporate tax (%)	Total tax ($ millions)	Share of total tax (%)
16–23	130	0.4	3,151	0.8
24–31	573	1.8	27,683	7.4
32–39	1,195	3.8	45,653	12.2
40–47	3,442	11.0	96,416	25.8
48–55	4,604	14.7	85,177	22.8
56–63	5,703	18.2	51,799	13.9
64–71	6,862	21.9	30,365	8.1
72–79	5,695	18.2	21,126	5.7
80+	3,137	10.0	11,997	3.2

Source: The Fraser Institute's Canadian Tax Simulator 2003.

burden. As we can see, the results are very different depending on which assumptions one makes. How reasonable each assumption is depends on what we believe about the mobility of capital between corporate and non-corporate sectors and between Canada and the rest of the world. The more mobile capital is, the less of the burden of the tax it will bear. There is an active debate over the degree to which capital can pass the tax on to

Figure 7.2: Shares of total tax and corporate tax paid (%), by age group, 2003

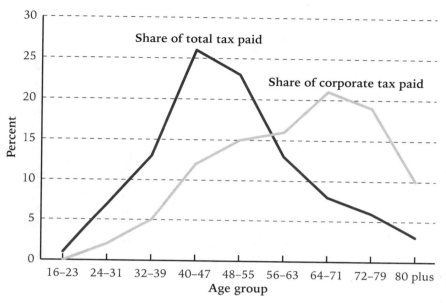

Source: The Fraser Institute's Canadian Tax Simulator 2003.

labour—a debate that we cannot resolve here. The point to keep in mind is that it is people who pay the corporate tax. Under two of the three possible scenarios (capital bears all, capital and labour bear equally) the elderly pay significantly for a policy that is widely touted as a tax on the "rich."

The myth of the untaxed corporation

By now, it should be clear that the incidence of corporate tax is complex and that brash claims about it have to be examined cautiously. One particularly brash claim that often receives great attention from the Press is that some corporations in Canada are not paying their fair share of taxes. In particular, a labour-sponsored study claimed that 81,462 profitable corporations in Canada paid no taxes on profits of nearly $17.1 billion in 1994 and, as a result, have forced ordinary Canadians to shoulder a larger responsibility for paying the nation's taxes (British Columbia Federation of Labour 1997).

A study by the Ontario NDP government's Fair Tax Commission shows a different picture. The Fair Tax Commission analyzed a special 1989 survey of 177,000 corporations in Ontario and reached the following conclusions.

Figure 7.3: Corporate tax as a percentage of average taxes paid by age group in 2003 under three incidence assumptions

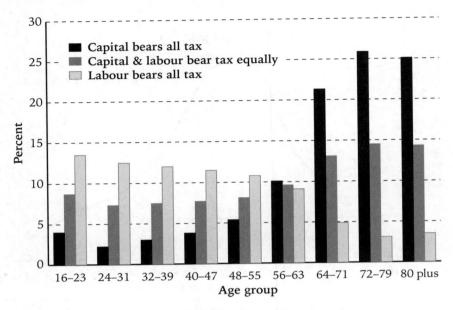

Source: The Fraser Institute's Canadian Tax Simulator 2003.

- 54% of the profits that were not taxed were inter-corporate dividends or equity income earned by subsidiaries. That is, profits earned by one branch of the corporation were transferred, after they had been taxed, to another part of the corporation. Taxing these transfers of money would be like taxing a person for moving his wallet from one pocket to another.

- 31% of profits were exempt either because they were used to replace depreciating equipment or because they were "paper gains," that is, assets transferred between members of the same corporate group without any economic gain or loss to the group.

- 11% of the profits not subject to tax were earned by firms that had lost money in the previous year. The tax system takes the long view of profits and allows firms to carry their losses forward. If a corporation lost $1 million last year and earned $1 million this year, over two years it has not made any profit and so should not be taxed within this two-year cycle.

- 4% of profits were exempt from taxation because of the temporary small-business tax holiday.

In other words, in the view of the NDP government in Ontario at the time, the survey of corporations suggested that corporations were not unfairly avoiding taxes.

Those advocating new or increased corporate taxes and claiming that corporations are getting an "easy ride" avoid statistics that show that, in recent years, corporations pay significantly more than they did in the past. Table 7.1 shows that, when we remove the effects of inflation, corporations contribute significantly more to tax revenue now than they did in the 1960s. These critics focus on the proportion of corporate taxes in total taxes collected by government, which has fallen sharply since the 1950s and 1960s. This is deceptive because, as table 7.4 shows, while corporate tax revenues as a percent of total tax revenues have fallen by 39.7% between 1961 and 2002, corporate taxes as a share of GDP have fallen by only 12.6%. Even though governments now get a smaller fraction of their revenues from corporations than they did in 1961, this has been caused by the unprecedented growth in personal taxation that we described earlier in the book and not by corporations cheating the tax system. Table 7.4 also shows that direct taxes on persons as a percent of total tax revenue increased by 50.8% from 1961 to 2002 and that direct taxes on persons as a percent of GDP increased by 118.5%.

Yet another perspective on the claim that corporations are not paying their fair share of tax comes from the work of economist Alan Douglas (Douglas 1990). He performed a subtle exercise to find the reasons that the corporate tax has declined as a share of total government revenue. He found that falling profits were the most significant reason

Table 7.4: Importance of corporate and personal income taxes in government tax revenues

Levied on:	Direct taxes as a percent of total tax revenues			Direct taxes as a percent of GDP		
	1961	2002	Change (%) 1961–2002	1961	2002	Change (%) 1961–2002
Corporations	17.0	10.3	(39.7)	4.0	3.5	(12.6)
Persons	23.5	35.4	50.8	5.5	12.0	118.5

Sources: Statistics Canada, National Economic and Financial Accounts; calculations by the authors.

Table 7.5: Canadian corporate taxes

	GDP ($millions)	Corporate* profits before taxes ($millions)	Corporate* profits before tax as a percent of GDP
1961	41,253	4,498	10.9
1964	52,653	6,383	12.1
1967	69,834	7,697	11.0
1970	90,367	8,860	9.8
1973	129,196	16,888	13.1
1976	200,296	22,667	11.3
1979	280,309	38,822	13.8
1982	379,859	29,206	7.7
1985	485,714	54,665	11.3
1988	613,094	71,720	11.7
1991	685,367	38,099	5.6
1994	770,873	71,291	9.2
1997	882,733	94,585	10.7
2000	1,075,566	147,490	13.7
2001	1,107,459	137,171	12.4
2002	1,154,949	143,430	12.4

Sources: Statistics Canada; calculations by the authors.
*Includes government business enterprises.

for the decline: "if the profit rate for 1976 to 1985 had remained at its 1966–1975 average of 11.01% ... average [annual government] revenue would have been $11.31 billion instead of $7.55 billion. An extra $27.6 billion in corporate taxes would have been collected over the decade" (Douglas 1990: 70).

Table 7.5 supports this result: in almost every year shown, when corporate profits as a share of GDP increased, corporate taxes as a percent of total taxes increased. The converse is also true. Mr. Douglas found, in addition, that tax breaks, such as accelerated depreciation, reduced tax revenues much less than did declining profitability. Many of these tax breaks were eliminated in 1987 in any case. Until recently, corporations in Canada had known a long slide in profitability. Governments have not "taken it easy" on these corporations. Rather, it is simply that corporations have become a less lucrative and less reliable source of revenue than individual workers.

Direct taxes from corporations* ($millions)	Corporate taxes as a percentage of profits	Corporate* tax as a percent of total tax revenue
1,649	36.7	17.0
2,101	32.9	16.4
2,396	31.1	12.8
3,070	34.7	11.6
5,079	30.1	13.1
7,128	31.4	11.8
10,038	25.9	12.7
11,755	40.2	9.9
15,563	28.5	10.5
17,586	24.5	8.6
15,015	39.4	6.1
19,342	27.1	7.1
32,250	34.1	10.0
48,139	32.6	12.5
37,837	27.6	9.8
40,350	28.1	10.3

The fact that taxes upon corporations' profits depend upon the relative uncertainty of corporate profits is probably the main reason for the growing popularity of taxes upon corporate capital among the provinces. In 1987, four provinces imposed capital taxes on corporations and seven imposed capital taxes on banks. In 1999, only three provinces did not impose corporate capital taxes and all provinces taxed bank capital. The corporate capital tax generates revenue for the government by assessing a levy on corporations based on the amount of capital (essentially debt and equity) employed. Because it penalizes industries like software, biotechnology, and communications that make an intensive use of capital, the corporate capital tax may be the most damaging tax in Canada. (For more information on corporate capital taxes, see Clemens et al. 2002). While many provinces and the federal government have made a commitment to eliminating capital taxes over the course of the next five years, many provinces—most notably Saskatchewan and Quebec—still raise a significant portion of their revenue from capital taxes (Clemens 2002).

Chapter 8
Canada and the Rest
of the World

SO FAR, WE HAVE CONCENTRATED OUR ATTENTION on how much tax Canadians pay and how those taxes have been changing. This is useful information if one wants to compare Canada today with Canada in the past. It is sufficient to concentrate on the tax burden within our own country provided one is fairly isolated from the rest of the world. However, new technology and falling trade barriers are weaving the economies of the world closer together than they have ever been before and stripping away any efforts at isolation. This means that, when we consider our taxes, we also have to look at the tax rates and levels in the countries with which we have close ties.

How do we compare?
The Canadian tax system is complex and no single number can summarize it. The same is true of comparisons between Canada and the rest of the world. Foreign tax systems are different and governments abroad provide their citizens with different levels of services. This means that comparing the total amount of taxes paid in Canada and in, say, Japan may tell us little about whether taxes are too high in one country relative to the other. For example, Canada may tax more than other countries but it may provide more and better public services. That is, the tax price of government activity may be lower here. This sort of subtlety does not

mean, however, that international comparisons are meaningless. There are some numbers that can give us a broad feel for the differences between the systems.

The level of taxes

Figure 8.1 shows the total amount of tax in Canada and other industrialized nations as a percentage of GDP in 2000. The horizontal bar for each country is divided into five sections: income and profit taxes; social security taxes; property taxes; goods and services taxes; and other taxes. Table 8.1 shows the numerical breakdown of the relative importance of each tax category. The comparison shows that Canada ranks third lowest in terms of taxes paid as a percentage of GDP. However, it collects significantly more taxes as a portion of its economy—35.8% of GDP—than second-place United States, where taxes absorb on 29.6% of GDP. A closer look reveals that Canada has the second highest income and profit taxes as a percentage of total taxes, the lowest social security taxes, and high property taxes. Some claim that these low social security taxes give Can-

Figure 8.1: International comparison of taxes paid as a percentage of GDP, 2000

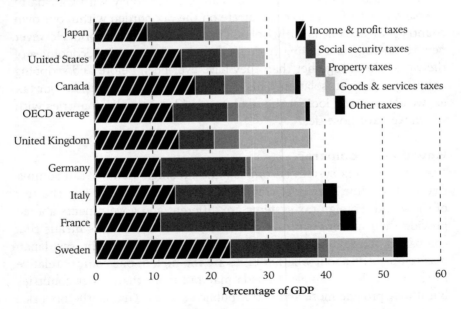

Source: OECD, Revenue Statistics, 1965–2001, 2002.

Table 8.1: International tax comparisons, 2000

	Total tax as a percent of GDP	Taxes as a percent of total taxes				
		Income and Profits	Social Security	Property	Goods & Services	Other
Japan	27.1	34.1	36.5	10.3	18.9	0.3
United States	29.6	50.9	23.3	10.1	15.7	0.0
Canada	35.8	49.0	14.3	9.7	24.4	2.7
United Kingdom	37.4	39.0	16.4	11.9	32.3	0.0
OECD average	37.4	36.0	24.8	5.4	31.6	1.9
Germany	37.9	30.1	39.0	2.3	28.1	0.0
Italy	42.0	33.2	28.5	4.3	28.4	5.3
France	45.3	25.0	36.1	6.8	25.8	6.0
Sweden	54.2	43.2	28.1	3.4	20.7	4.4

Source: OECD, Revenue Statistics, 1965–2001, 2002.

ada room to raise contribution rates but they miss certain facts. Canada's population is comparatively young so our social security taxes should be low. Japan has a relatively old population and social security taxes there are over one third of the total tax bill. Canada Pension Plan contributions have already increased from the 1997 rate of 6.0% to 9.4% in 2002 and are scheduled to increase to 9.9% this year (2003).

Canada's overall tax burden since 1965 has been rising rapidly. Table 8.2 shows that the percentage increase in our taxes as a share of GDP from 1965 to 2000 was 39.8%

Canada's debt is a hidden tax that does not come out in this international comparison of visible taxes. Table 8.3 shows Canada's government debt as a fraction of GDP and compares it to other industrialized countries. Among the 19 OECD countries that report comparable debt statistics, 9 have lower ratio of debt to GDP than Canada (OECD 2003).

Why bother comparing?

Comparing taxes is interesting because it indicates how well a country can compete in the international marketplace. Taxes raise the costs facing a business and, if there is no offsetting movement in the exchange rate, they may cripple its ability to undersell foreign competitors who come from countries with lower tax burdens. We must be careful before jumping to conclusions, however, because in return for paying taxes we receive

Table 8.2: Change in taxes as a percentage of GDP, 1965–2000

	Total change (%)	Change by tax type (%)			
		Profit & Income	Social security	Property	Goods & Services
United States	19.8	26.9	109.1	(23.1)	(16.1)
Germany	19.9	6.5	74.1	(50.0)	1.9
United Kingdom	23.0	29.2	29.8	0.0	19.8
France	31.3	105.5	39.0	106.7	(11.4)
Canada	39.8	76.8	264.3	(2.8)	(16.3)
OECD average	45.0	51.1	102.1	0.0	19.6
Japan	48.1	15.0	147.5	86.7	6.3
Sweden	54.9	21.9	261.9	216.7	2.8
Italy	64.7	202.2	36.8	0.0	17.8

Source: OECD, Revenue Statistics, 1965–2001, 2002.

Table 8.3: Net government debt as a percentage of GDP, 2003 (estimate)

Norway	(93.4)	Canada	36.9
Finland	(46.0)	Netherlands	41.3
Sweden	(4.7)	France	42.3
Denmark	4.4	United States	47.1
Australia	4.8	Germany	50.3
New Zealand	18.0	Japan	80.2
United Kingdom	29.4	Italy	95.7

Source: OECD, *OECD Economic Outlook*, No. 73, June 2003.

government services that help us to be productive. Infrastructures such as roads, schools, and legal and penal systems that work as they should are all vital aids to success in facing the challenge of foreign competition. This means that we have to ask whether a rapidly rising tax burden represents heavier investments in these productive infrastructures. It is imaginable that a higher tax burden does not represent a competitive disadvantage provided those taxes are being spent productively by government.

The evidence from 1966 to 2002 shows that the fraction of government budgets spent on these vital infrastructures is falling in Canada (table 8.4). A greater fraction of our tax dollar is going to finance interest payments on the debt and social service programs. These expenditures make up close to three-quarters of government budgets. A similar picture emerges for many of the foreign countries with which we have been comparing Canada in this chapter. Two economists from the International Monetary Fund, Vito Tanzi and Ludger Schuknecht, report in a book published by the Fraser Institute that average government spending in 17 industrialized countries rose from 28% to 46% between 1960 and 1996. Further, they reported that countries with "small" government sectors (public expenditure less than 40% of GDP) do not have worse indicators of social and economic well-being than countries with "big" governments (public expenditure greater than 50% of GDP) and that these "small" government countries often achieve better results (Grubel 1998). Results published elsewhere by the same authors (Tanzi and Schuknecht 1995) show that, between 1960 and 1994, average spending on interest payments in the 17 industrialized countries studied increased from 1.9% to 4.3% of GDP and average spending on subsidies and transfers increased from 8.3% to 23.0% of GDP. What this means is that, when we are comparing tax levels, it is right to think that a higher tax burden may make a country less competitive because much of the increase in the tax burden in Canada and other industrialized countries over the past four decades is due to government activities that do not enhance the productivity of a nation.

Canada and the United States

The United States buys about 85% of Canada's exports. The proximity of the United States and the increasing flow of goods and services over our border because of NAFTA means that it is the tax system of the United States with which we ought particularly to compare our tax system. The OECD estimates that Canadian governments collected 30% more revenue (as a percentage of GDP) than their American counterparts in 2002 (OECD 2003). The OECD, in a recent country survey for Canada, noted the following.

> Despite the significant reductions enacted, personal income tax rates remain higher in Canada than in the United States (except for the lowest incomes). The US tax cuts proposed by the Administration, if fully implemented, would broadly re-establish the previously existing personal income tax gap between Canada and the United States. (OECD 2001: 59)

Table 8.4: Composition of total government spending, 1965/1966

	1965/1966	
	$millions	% of total
General services	966	5.6
Protection of persons & property	2,268	13.2
Transportation & communication	2,149	12.5
Health	1,678	9.8
Social services	3,112	18.1
Education	2,982	17.3
Resource conservation and industrial development	870	5.1
Environment	435	2.5
Recreation & Culture	257	1.5
Labour, Employment and Immigration	51	0.3
Housing	23	0.1
Foreign affairs and international assistance	159	0.9
Regional planning & development	80	0.5
Research establishments	68	0.4
Transfers to own enterprises	270	1.6
Debt charges	1,718	10.0
Other Expenditures	122	0.7
Total expenditures	17,207	100.0

Sources: Statistics Canada, Public Finance Historical Data, 1965/66-1991/92, catalogue calculations by the authors.

The disincentive imposed on investment by corporate taxes and other taxes on business income tends to be relatively high for large firms. Duanjie Chen and Kenneth McKenzie found that the marginal effective tax rate on investment in manufacturing was higher in Canada than in all the countries studied except Germany and Japan. (Chen and McKenzie 1996). Similar patterns prevailed for services, with the differential between Canada and the United States, in particular, being even larger.

and 2002/2003

2002/2003		Percentage point change 1965/1966–2002/2003
$millions	% of total	
15.646	3.4	(2.3)
35,775	7.7	(5.5)
19,848	4.3	(8.2)
81,720	17.6	7.8
145,471	31.3	13.2
65,002	14.0	(3.4)
16,260	3.5	(1.6)
9,795	2.1	(0.4)
11,140	2.4	0.9
2,929	0.6	0.3
3,956	0.8	0.7
4,751	1.0	0.1
1,955	0.4	0.0
1,899	0.4	0.0
n/a	n/a	n/a
48,738	10.5	0.5
579	0.1	(0.6)
465,462	100.0	0.0

68-512; Financial Management System data from the Public Institutions Division;

Compared to our main trading partner, the United States, our tax rates and levels are high. Compared to other industrialized countries, our debt burden and resultant interest costs as a share of total government spending are high. These fiscal weaknesses detract from Canada's international competitiveness and are especially important in the face of falling trade barriers and increasing global competition.

Calculate How Much
Tax You Really Pay

THIS SECTION IS A SIMPLE TOOL that will help you discover how much tax you really pay. It takes some work but arriving at the final result requires only a few minutes and some calculator strokes. The tables that follow show what are known as "regression estimates" of the tax system. We have tried to relate how much tax families pay to characteristics such as age and sex of the head of the family, size of the family, and level of income. The formulas that we have developed will give you an approximate idea of your total taxes.

The sample calculation on the following page demonstrates how you would proceed if you were a 45-year-old male head of a family of four living in Newfoundland, with a family income of $50,000. The column under "Coefficient," which we provide, is used to multiply the column "You," which you complete with your personal characteristics. This gives a column called "Multiple," which is then summed (including what we provide as an adjustment factor). The sum is an estimate of your family's total tax bill. We provide these tables for all 10 provinces.

Sample calculation

Characteristics	Coefficient (1)	You (2)	Multiple (1) × (2)
Number of children	−139	× 2	= −278
Age of Head	−16	× 45	= −720
Sex of Head (0 if male; 1 if female)	−385	× 0	= 0
Married or common-law (0 if no; 1 if yes)	−1,119	× 1	= −1,119
Family Income	0.49	× 50,000	= 24,500
Square of Family Income	5.4×10^{-8}	× $(50,000)^2$	= 134
Adjustment Factor	−1,218		= −1,218
Total			= 21,299

Newfoundland and Labrador

Characteristics	Coefficient (1)	You (2)	Multiple (1) x (2)
Number of children	−139	× _____	= _____
Age of Head	−16	× _____	= _____
Sex of Head (0 if male; 1 if female)	−385	× _____	= _____
Married or common-law (0 if no; 1 if yes)	−1,119	× _____	= _____
Family Income	0.49	× _____	= _____
Square of Family Income	5.4×10^{-8}	× (_____)²	= _____
Adjustment Factor	−1,218		= −1,218
Total			= _____

Prince Edward Island

Characteristics	Coefficient (1)	You (2)	Multiple (1) x (2)
Number of children	−503	× _____	= _____
Age of Head	−15	× _____	= _____
Sex of Head (0 if male; 1 if female)	−71	× _____	= _____
Married or common-law (0 if no; 1 if yes)	−1,859	× _____	= _____
Family Income	0.45	× _____	= _____
Square of Family Income	8.3×10^{-7}	× (_____)²	= _____
Adjustment Factor	−701		= −701
Total			= _____

Nova Scotia

Characteristics	Coefficient (1)	You (2)	Multiple (1) x (2)
Number of children	−158	× _____	= _____
Age of Head	3	× _____	= _____
Sex of Head (0 if male; 1 if female)	−12	× _____	= _____
Married or common-law (0 if no; 1 if yes)	−1,930	× _____	= _____
Family Income	0.53	× _____	= _____
Square of Family Income	-1.6×10^{-7}	× (_____)^2	= _____
Adjustment Factor	−1,819		= −1,819
Total			= _____

New Brunswick

Characteristics	Coefficient (1)	You (2)	Multiple (1) x (2)
Number of children	−240	× _____	= _____
Age of Head	−23	× _____	= _____
Sex of Head (0 if male; 1 if female)	−397	× _____	= _____
Married or common-law (0 if no; 1 if yes)	−1,413	× _____	= _____
Family Income	0.49	× _____	= _____
Square of Family Income	1.9×10^{-7}	× (_____)^2	= _____
Adjustment Factor	−104		= −104
Total			= _____

Quebec

Characteristics	Coefficient (1)	You (2)	Multiple (1) x (2)
Number of children	−1,091	× _____	= _____
Age of Head	−37	× _____	= _____
Sex of Head (0 if male; 1 if female)	−55	× _____	= _____
Married or common-law (0 if no; 1 if yes)	−2,350	× _____	= _____
Family Income	0.57	× _____	= _____
Square of Family Income	3.0×10^{-7}	× (_____)^2	= _____
Adjustment Factor	−749		= −749
Total			= _____

Ontario

Characteristics	Coefficient (1)	You (2)	Multiple (1) x (2)
Number of children	−295	× _____	= _____
Age of Head	−22	× _____	= _____
Sex of Head (0 if male; 1 if female)	−54	× _____	= _____
Married or common-law (0 if no; 1 if yes)	−1,316	× _____	= _____
Family Income	0.49	× _____	= _____
Square of Family Income	2.8×10^{-7}	× (_____)^2	= _____
Adjustment Factor	39		= 39
Total			= _____

Manitoba

Characteristics	Coefficient (1)	You (2)	Multiple (1) x (2)
Number of children	−635	× _____	= _____
Age of Head	−22	× _____	= _____
Sex of Head (0 if male; 1 if female)	−274	× _____	= _____
Married or common-law (0 if no; 1 if yes)	−1,538	× _____	= _____
Family Income	0.52	× _____	= _____
Square of Family Income	4.6×10^{-8}	× (_____)^2	= _____
Adjustment Factor	−305		= −305
Total			= _____

Saskatchewan

Characteristics	Coefficient (1)	You (2)	Multiple (1) x (2)
Number of children	−267	× _____	= _____
Age of Head	−17	× _____	= _____
Sex of Head (0 if male; 1 if female)	−103	× _____	= _____
Married or common-law (0 if no; 1 if yes)	−1,487	× _____	= _____
Family Income	0.52	× _____	= _____
Square of Family Income	1.1×10^{-7}	× (_____)^2	= _____
Adjustment Factor	−946		= −946
Total			= _____

Alberta

Characteristics	Coefficient	You	Multiple
	(1)	(2)	(1) x (2)
Number of children	−6	× _____	= _____
Age of Head	−18	× _____	= _____
Sex of Head (0 if male; 1 if female)	−81	× _____	= _____
Married or common-law (0 if no; 1 if yes)	−1,498	× _____	= _____
Family Income	0.5	× _____	= _____
Square of Family Income	-6.5×10^{-8}	× (_____)^2	= _____
Adjustment Factor	−1,104		= −1,104
Total			= _____

British Columbia

Characteristics	Coefficient	You	Multiple
	(1)	(2)	(1) x (2)
Number of children	−47	× _____	= _____
Age of Head	−11	× _____	= _____
Sex of Head (0 if male; 1 if female)	−78	× _____	= _____
Married or common-law (0 if no; 1 if yes)	−719	× _____	= _____
Family Income	0.53	× _____	= _____
Square of Family Income	-7.3×10^{-8}	× (_____)^2	= _____
Adjustment Factor	−688		= −688
Total			= _____

Glossary of Principal Terms, Measures, and Concepts

Indices

Index An index is a method of measuring the percentage changes from a base year of a certain item, such as the price, volume, or value of food or the dollar amount of taxes. In order to construct an index, the price, volume, or value of the particular item being indexed in each year is divided by the price, volume, or value of the item in the base year; it is then multiplied by 100. An index has a value of 100 in the base year. In this book, the base year is 1961.

Consumer Price Index The Consumer Price Index measures the percentage change from a base year in the cost of purchasing a constant "basket" of goods and services representing the purchases by a particular population group in a specified time period. The Consumer Price Index (CPI) reflects price movements of some 300 items. The CPI is calculated monthly by Statistics Canada (see below).

Consumer Tax Index The Consumer Tax Index measures the percentage change from a base year in the average Canadian family's tax bill. The Consumer Tax Index (CTI) is composed of federal, provincial, and municipal taxes. The CTI, calculated by The Fraser Institute, was introduced by the Institute for the first time in the first edition of *Tax Facts*, which was entitled *How Much Tax Do You Really Pay?*

Balanced Budget Tax Index   The Balanced Budget Tax Index is the same as the *Consumer Tax Index* except that also included in the calculation is the amount of tax that would have to be raised if governments did not issue debt and were, in fact, balancing their budgets. This index was introduced by The Fraser Institute for the first time in the second edition of the *Tax Facts* series, *Tax Facts: The Canadian Consumer Tax Index and You*.

Statistical terms

Average Canadian Family   The average Canadian family represents a family that had average income in a particular year. The averages were constructed from Statistics Canada's expenditure and income surveys, details of which appear in the bibliography.

Family   A family is a group of persons dependent upon a common or pooled income for their major expenditure items and living in the same dwelling. The term also applies to a financially independent unattached individual living alone.

Family Expenditure Survey   The *Family Expenditure Survey* refers to the surveys published by Statistics Canada that show patterns of family expenditure for Canada by selected characteristics such as urban or rural area, family type, life cycle, income, age of head, tenure, occupation of head, education of head, country of origin and year an immigrant arrived in Canada. This survey has been replaced by the *Survey of Household Spending* (see below).

Shelter expenditure   Shelter expenditure is included as one of the selected expenditure items in this book. It refers to expenditures on rented or owned living quarters or repairs to these quarters. Mortgage interest and payments of principal on owned living quarters and expenditures on water and heating fuel are included. The definition of shelter changed beginning in the 1997 reference year; for more information on this change, see Statistics Canada 2002.

Social Policy Simulation Database and Model (SPSD/M)   The SPSD/M is a static microsimulation model that comprises a database, a series of tax/transfer algorithms and models, analytical software, and user docu-

mentation. The SPSD/M is a tool designed to analyze the financial inter-
actions of governments with individuals and families in Canada. It allows
estimation of the income redistributive effects or cost implications of
changes in the personal taxation and cash transfer system.

Statistics Canada   Statistics Canada is Canada's official statistical agency, often referred to as "StatsCan." Statistics Canada provided much of
the published and unpublished data for this book. For a detailed listing of
these sources, see *Government sources*, in References.

Survey of Consumer Finances   The *Survey of Consumer Finances* refers to
the survey from Statistics Canada that gives details of the incomes and
characteristics of families. Information is given on the incomes (from,
e.g., salaries, wages, and pensions) of the head of family and of the
spouse, residence (*e.g.*, province, rural or urban), personal characteristics
(*e.g.* size of family, age and educational level of head and spouse), and
labour-related characteristics (*e.g.* occupation, employment status). This
survey has been replaced by the *Survey of Labour and Income Dynamics* (see
below).

Survey of Household Spending (SHS)   The *Survey of Household Spending*
collects information on how much money households across the country spend on various items such as food, shelter, clothing, entertainment,
transportation, health care, and other items. This survey includes households of all sizes, be it an individual or a family. The sample for this survey is approximately 24,000 households.

Survey of Labour and Income Dynamics (SLID)   The *Survey of Labour and
Income Dynamics* (SLID) is a longitudinal survey of households conducted
by Statistics Canada. It is designed to capture changes in the economic
well-being of individuals and families over time and the determinants of
their well-being. Individuals originally selected for the survey are interviewed once or twice per year for six years to collect information about
their experiences in the labour market, income, and family circumstances.
In order to obtain complete information on families and to obtain cross-
sectional data, people who live with the original respondents at any time
during the six years are also interviewed during the time of cohabitation.
The sample for this survey is approximately 35,000 households.

Income concepts

Cash income   Cash income is the income that a family would report when completing a government survey, such as the *Survey of Household Spending*, the *Survey of Labour and Income Dynamics*, or the Census form. It includes income that one receives regularly, such as salary or wage income (before tax) and payments from government such as old age security, employment insurance, and family allowances. Families generally under-report their income so the estimates of cash income used in this study are "bumped up" using a Statistics Canada adjustment to include income that is often omitted when a family reports its income. Income that is often excluded is bond or bank interest and dividend income.

Deciles   Deciles are a way of categorizing families. All families were arranged according to total income before tax, from lowest income to highest, and then divided into ten groups, i.e. the first decile contains the 10% of families with the lowest incomes, the second decile contains the 10% of families with the second lowest incomes, and so on.

Hidden income   Hidden income is income that a family receives but probably does not consider to be a part of its income. Hidden income is largely made up of employers' contributions to pension plans, medical premiums, and insurance plans. Another example is imputed non-farm rent. (For a more complete discussion of imputed non-farm rent, see The Fraser Institute's publication, *Rent Control—A Popular Paradox*, p. 33).

Income from government   Income from government is income that a family receives as payment from the government, whereas taxes are payments to the government. Therefore, income from the government can be considered a "negative tax." It is often referred to as a transfer payment. It includes such items as the Canada Child Tax Benefit (CCTB), old age security payments, veterans' grants, and so on.

Total income before tax   Total income before tax is the term used in this book to designate the amount of income the family would have received before paying tax. It is composed of cash income, which includes income from government (transfer payments), and hidden income.

Transfer payments, see *Income from government* above.

About taxes

Balanced budget tax rate   The balanced budget tax rate is the tax rate that Canadians would face if governments had to balance their budgets and finance all expenditures from current tax revenue instead of issuing debt.

Corporate profits tax   Corporate profits tax is the tax paid on the profits of a corporation. This is also referred to as the "corporate income tax."

Deferred taxation   Deferred taxation is the debt incurred by the various levels of government to finance the expenditures that cannot be met by current tax revenue. It is, in effect, deferred taxation because the debts and the interest on them must ultimately be paid out of future tax revenue.

Direct taxes   Direct taxes are taxes that are paid directly by the family. Examples of direct taxes are the personal income tax and property taxes. They are often referred to as explicit taxes.

Hidden taxes   Hidden taxes are taxes that are concealed in the price of articles that one buys. Hidden taxes are also referred to as implicit taxes. The most well-known form of the hidden tax is the indirect tax. Examples of hidden taxes are the tobacco, fuel, and alcohol taxes and import duties.

Negative tax, see *Income from government* above.

Progressive, proportional, regressive   Progressive, proportional, and regressive are terms that refer to the proportionality of taxes on income. A tax is called proportional if it takes the same fraction of income from those with a low income as it does from those with a high income. Employment Insurance payments and Canada Pension payments up to the maximum earnings level are examples of proportional taxes.

A progressive tax is one that takes a greater proportion of income from those with a high income than from those with a low income (income tax, for example).

A regressive tax is one that takes a greater proportion of income from those with a low income than it does from those with a high income (sales tax, for example).

Social security taxes   Social security taxes comprise both federal and provincial taxes. The federal category includes employers' and employees' contributions to public service pensions and to Employment Insurance. Provincial social security taxes include employers' and employees' contributions to public service pensions and Workers' Compensation. Also included in this category as taxes are payments to the Canada and Quebec Pension Plans and medical and hospital insurance premiums.

Tax burden   The tax burden is the means of determining who ultimately pays tax and is synonymous with the term "tax incidence." Tax burden is measured by the decline in real purchasing power that results from the imposition of a tax.

Powers of taxation under the Constitution of Canada   The general scheme of taxation in the Constitution Act, 1982 can be summarized in this way:

- the federal government is given an unlimited power to tax.

- the provinces are also given what amounts to an unlimited power to tax "within the province;" that is to say, an unlimited power to tax persons within their jurisdiction and to impose taxes in respect to property located, and income earned, within the province. But their taxing powers are framed in such a way as to preclude them from imposing taxes that would have the effect of creating barriers to interprovincial trade and, generally, from taxing persons and property outside the province.

References

Alexander, Jared, and Joel Emes (1998). *Canadian Government Debt: A Guide to the Indebtedness of Canada and the Provinces*. Critical Issues Bulletin. Vancouver, BC: The Fraser Institute.

Bethune, Brian A. (1993). The Competitiveness of the Canadian Tax System. *Canadian Tax Journal* 41, 6: 1119–27.

Bird, Richard M. (1970). Growth of Government Spending in Canada. Toronto, ON: Canadian Tax Foundation.

British Columbia Federation of Labour (1997). Corporate Tax Freedom Day. Press release (January 28).

Boucher, Michel (1998). *Évaluation de la perfomance du government du Parti québécois 1994–1998*. Communication sur des points cruciaux. Vancouver, BC: The Fraser Institute.

Browning, Edgar K. (1978). The Burden of Taxation. *Journal of Political Economy* 86, 4 (August): 649–71.

Browning, Edgar K., and William R. Johnson (1979). *The Distribution of the Tax Burden*. Washington, DC: American Enterprise Institute.

Burrows, Marie. *Fiscal Positions of the Provinces: The 1983 Budgets*. Conference Board of Canada; Aeric Inc.

Campbell, Harry F. 1975). An Input-Output Analysis of the Commodity Structure of Indirect Taxes in Canada. *Canadian Journal of Economics* (August): 433.

Canadian Bankers Association (1998). *Canadian Bank Facts, 1997/98*.

Canadian Institute of Actuaries (1995). *Troubled Tomorrows: The Report of the Institute of Actuaries' Task Force on Retirement Savings* (January).

Canadian Tax Foundation (various issues). *The National Finances: An Analysis of the Revenues and Expenditures of the Government of Canada.*
——— (various issues). *Provincial and Municipal Finances.* Toronto, ON: Canadian Tax Foundation.

Chen, Duanjie, and Kenneth J. McKenzie (1996). The Impact of Taxation on Capital Markets: An International Comparison of Effective Tax Rates on Capital. Prepared for Capital Market Issues, a conference sponsored by Industry Canada.

Chera, Satinder, and Fazil Mihlar (1998). *The Government of British Columbia, 1991–1998: An Assessment of Performance and a Blueprint for Economic Recovery.* Critical Issues Bulletin. Vancouver, BC: The Fraser Institute.

Clemens, Jason, and Joel Emes (2001). *Returning British Columbia to Prosperity.* Public Policy Sources 47. Vancouver, BC: The Fraser Institute.

Clemens, Jason, Joel Emes, and Rodger Scott (2002). *The Corporate Capital Tax: Canada's Most Damaging Tax.* Public Policy Sources 56. Vancouver, BC: The Fraser Institute.

Clemens, Jason (2002). The Big News is No News on the Corporate Capital Tax. *Fraser Forum* (November): 31–32.

Clemens, Jason, Amela Karabegovic, and Niels Veldhuis (2003). *Ontario Prosperity: Is Best of Second Best Good Enough?* Studies in Economic Prosperity 1. Vancouver, BC: The Fraser Institute.

Conference Board of Canada (1996). *Provincial Outlook* 11, 2 (Spring).

Cathy Cotton, Kevin Bishop, Phil Giles, Peter Hewer, and Yves Saint-Pierre (1999). *A Comparison of the Results of the Survey of Labour and Income Dynamics (SLID) and the Survey of Consumer Finances (SCF), 1993–1997: Update.* Ottawa: Statistics Canada.

Davies, James, France St.-Hilaire, and John Whalley (1984). Some Calculations of Lifetime Tax Incidence. *American Economic Review* 74, 4 (September): 633–49.

Dodge, David A. (1975). Impact of Tax, Transfer and Expenditure Policies of Government on the Distribution of Personal Incomes in Canada. *Review of Income and Wealth* 21, 1 (March): 1–52.

Douglas, Alan V. (1990). Changes in Corporate Tax Revenue. *Canadian Tax Journal* 38, 1 (Jan./Feb.): 66–81.

Emes, Joel F. (2001). January Questions and Answers. *Fraser Forum* (January): 13–15.

——— (2002). April Questions and Answers. *Fraser Forum* (April): 25–26.

Gillespie, W. Irwin (1966). *Incidence of Taxes and Public Expenditures in the Canadian Economy*. Studies of the Royal Commission on Taxation 2.

———— (1978). *In Search of Robin Hood*. Toronto, ON: C.D. Howe Institute.

Goffman, Irving J. (1972). *The Burden of Canadian Taxation*. Tax Paper 29 (July). Toronto, ON: Canadian Tax Foundation.

Grubel, Herbert G., ed. (1998). *How to Use the Fiscal Surplus: What Is the Optimal Size of Government?* Vancouver, BC: The Fraser Institute.

Horry, Isabella D., and Michael A. Walker (1994). *Government Spending Facts 2*. Vancouver, BC: The Fraser Institute.

Jones, Laura, and Stephen Graf (2001). *Canada's Regulatory Burden*. Fraser Forum, Special Issue (August). Vancouver, BC: The Fraser Institute.

La Forest, G.V. (1981). *The Allocation of Taxing Power under the Canadian Constitution*. Toronto, ON: Canadian Tax Foundation.

Law, Marc T., Howard I. Markowitz, and Fazil Mihlar (1997). *The Harris Government: A Mid-term Review*. Critical Issues Bulletin. Vancouver, BC: The Fraser Institute.

Lewis, Perrin (1978). The Tangled Tale of Taxes and Transfers. In Michael Walker (ed.), *Canadian Confederation at the Crossroads: The Search for a Federal-Provincial Balance* (Vancouver, BC: The Fraser Institute): 39–105.

Marx, Karl, and Friedrich Engels (1848). *Manifesto of the Communist Party*.

Maslove, Allan M. (1972). *The Pattern of Taxation in Canada*. Economic Council of Canada (December).

McGillivray, Don (1976). An Over-Simplified Look at Our Complicated Taxes. *Financial Times of Canada* (November 8).

McInnes, Craig (1996). Revenues Go Up in Smoke after Tobacco Tax Cuts. *Globe and Mail* (August 5).

Meerman, Jacob P. (1974). The Definition of Income in Studies of Budget Incidence and Income Distribution. *Review of Income and Wealth* 20, 4 (December): 512–22.

Mencken, H.L. (1989). *A New Dictionary of Quotations on Historical Principles from Ancient and Modern Times*. New York: Alfred A. Knopf.

Mihlar, Fazil (1998). *The Cost of Regulation in Canada, 1998 Edition*. Public Policy Sources 12. Vancouver, BC: The Fraser Institute.

Musgrave, Richard A., and Peggy B. Musgrave (1973). *Public Finance in Theory and Practice*. McGraw-Hill.

Organisation for Economic Cooperation and Development (1997a). *Agricultural Policies, Markets and Trade: Monitoring and Outlook, 1997*. Paris: OECD.

———— (1997b). *OECD Economic Surveys, Canada, 1997*. Paris: OECD.

———— (2001). *OECD Economic Surveys, Canada, 2001*. Paris: OECD.

———— (2002a). OECD *Economic Outlook* 72, 2002/2 (December). Paris: OECD.

———— (2002b). *Agricultural Policies in OECD Countries, Monitoring and Evaluation, 2002*. Paris: OECD.

———— (2002c). *Revenue Statistics 1965–2001*. Paris: OECD.

———— (2003). OECD *Economic Outlook* 73, 2003/3 (June). Paris: OECD.

Ort, Deborah L., and David B. Perry (2000). Provincial Budget Roundup. *Canadian Tax Journal* 48, 3: 710–33.

Pechman, Joseph A., and Benjamin A. Okner (1974). *Who Bears the Tax Burden? Studies of Government Finance*. Washington, DC: The Brookings Institute.

Perry, David B. (1997). *Financing the Canadian Federation, 1867 to 1995: Setting the Stage for Change*. Toronto, Ontario: Canadian Tax Foundation.

Perry, J. Harvey (1989). *A Fiscal History of Canada—The Postwar Years*. Toronto, ON: Canadian Tax Foundation.

Star, Spencer, and Sally C. Pipes (1976). *Income and Taxation in Canada 1961–1975*. Fraser Institute Technical Report 76–01. Vancouver, BC: The Fraser Institute.

Tanzi, Vito, and Ludger Schuknecht (1995). *The Growth of Government and the Reform of the State in Industrial Countries*. International Monetary Fund.

Treff, Karin, and David B. Perry (various years) *Finances of the Nation: A Review of Expenditures and Revenues of the Federal, Provincial, and Local Governments of Canada*. Toronto, ON: The Canadian Tax Foundation.

Usher, Dan (1995). *The Uneasy Case for Equalization Payments*. Vancouver, BC: The Fraser Institute.

Veldhuis, Niels, Joel Emes, Todd Fox and Raphael Barth (2003). *Canadian Government Debt 2003: A Guide to the Indebtedness of Canada and the Provinces*. Public Policy Sources 67. Vancouver, BC: The Fraser Institute.

Walker, Michael (ed.) (1976). *The Illusion of Wage and Price Control: Essays on Inflation, its Causes and its Cures*. Vancouver, BC: The Fraser Institute.

———— (1978). *Canadian Confederation at the Crossroads: The Search for a Federal-Provincial Balance*. Vancouver, BC: The Fraser Institute.

Watkins, G. Campbell, and Michael A. Walker (eds.) (1977). *Oil in the Seventies*. Vancouver, BC: The Fraser Institute.

_____ (eds.) (1981). *Reaction: The National Energy Program*. Vancouver, BC: The Fraser Institute.

Webber, Maryanne, Cathy Cotton, Mauri Meere, Kevin Bishop, and Peter Hewer (1999). *A Comparison of the Results of the Survey of Labour and Income Dynamics (SLID) and the Survey of Consumer Finances (SCF), 1993-1996*. Ottawa: Statistics Canada.

Wonnacott, Ronald J., and P. Wonnacott (1967). *Free Trade between the United States and Canada*. Cambridge, MA: Harvard University Press.

World Bank (2002). *World Development Indicators on CD-ROM, 2002*. Washington, D.C.: World Bank Publications.

World Trade Organization (2003). *Trade Policy Review, Canada, 2003*. Geneva, Switzerland: WTO Publications.

Zelder, Martin (2000). The Ultimate Health Care Reform. *Fraser Forum* (February): 15–16. Vancouver, BC: The Fraser Institute.

The Fraser Institute's series, Tax Facts

Walker, Michael, with Sally Pipes, John Raybould, and Spencer Star (1976). *How Much Tax Do You Really Pay? Your Real Tax Guide.*

Pipes, Sally, and Michael Walker (1979). *Tax Facts: The Canadian Consumer Tax Index and You.*

Pipes, Sally, and Michael Walker, with David Gill (1982). *Tax Facts 3: The Canadian Consumer Tax Index and You.*

Pipes, Sally, and Michael Walker, with Douglas Wills (1984). *Tax Facts 4: The Canadian Consumer Tax Index and You.*

_____ (1986). *Tax Facts 5: The Canadian Consumer Tax Index and You.*

Pipes, Sally, and Michael Walker, with Isabella Horry (1988). *Tax Facts 6: The Canadian Consumer Tax Index and You.*

Horry, Isabella, Sally Pipes, and Michael Walker (1990). *Tax Facts 7: The Canadian Consumer Tax Index and You.*

Horry, Isabella, Filip Palda, and Michael Walker (1992). *Tax Facts 8.*

_____ (1994). *Tax Facts 9.*

Horry, Isabella, Filip Palda, and Michael Walker, with Joel Emes (1997). *Tax Facts 10.*

Emes, Joel, and Michael Walker (1999). *Tax Facts 11.*

_____ (2001). *Tax Facts 12.*

Government sources

Bank of Canada (various issues). *Bank of Canada Review* (monthly).

Canada Customs and Revenue Agency, Income Statistics, 2002–2000 tax year. Available digitally at http://www.ccra-adrc.gc.ca.

Canada Customs and Revenue Agency, Income Statistics, 2003–2001 tax year. Available digitally at http://www.ccra-adrc.gc.ca.

Fair Tax Commission, Ontario (1992). Corporate Minimum Tax (March).

Department of Finance, Canada (1996). *The Budget Plan* (March 6).

Dominion Bureau of Statistics (1962). *Urban Family Expenditure 1962*.

Government of Canada (1867). *Constitution Act*.

Government of Canada, *House of Commons Debates* (1917). July 25: 3,765.

Revenue Canada (1995). *Tax Statistics on Individuals, 1993 Tax Year*.

Statistics Canada (1983). *Historical Statistics of Canada*. Second Edition. Ottawa: Supply and Services Canada.

Statistics Canada (1992). *Public Finance Historical Data, 1965/66–1991/92*. Cat. 68-512, occasional. Ottawa: Public Institutions Division.

Statistics Canada (1994a). *Local Government Revenue and Expenditure*. Ottawa: Public Institutions Division.

Statistics Canada (1994b). *Federal Government Revenue and Expenditure*. Ottawa: Public Institutions Division.

Statistics Canada (1994c). *Provincial Government Revenue and Expenditure*. Ottawa: Public Institutions Division.

Statistics Canada (1994d). Survey of Consumer Finances. Household Surveys Division. Unpublished Data.

Statistics Canada (1995a). *Agriculture Economic Statistics*. Cat. 21-603e, annual. Ottawa: Supply and Services Canada.

Statistics Canada (1995b). *Income Distribution by Size in Canada*. Cat. 13-207, annual. Ottawa: Household Surveys Division.

Statistics Canada (1995c). *Public Sector Finance, 1994–1995*. Cat. 68-212, annual. Ottawa: Public Institutions Division.

Statistics Canada (1996). *Public Sector Finance, 1995–1996*. Cat. 68-212-XPB. Ottawa: Public Institutions Division.

Statistics Canada (2000). *Income Trends in Canada 1980-1997*, on CD-ROM. Cat. 13F002XCB. Ottawa.

Statistics Canada (2001). Survey of Household Spending (SHS) 2001. Custom tabulation.

Statistics Canada (2002a). *Income Trends in Canada 1980-2000*, on CD-ROM. Cat. 13F002XCB. Ottawa.

Statistics Canada (2002b). *Population Projections*. Digital document: http://www.statcan.ca/english/Pgdb/demo23a.htm.

Statistics Canada (2002c). *Spending Patterns in Canada, 2002*. Cat. 62-202-XPE. Ottawa: Income Statistics Division.

Statistics Canada (various issues). *Canadian Economic Observer*. Cat. 11-010-XPB. Ottawa.

Statistics Canada (various issues). *The Consumer Price Index*. Cat. 62-001-XPB. Ottawa.

Statistics Canada (various issues). *National Economic and Financial Accounts*. Cat. 13-001-XPB. Ottawa: National Accounts and Environment Division.

Statistics Canada (various issues). *National Income and Expenditure Accounts*. Cat. 13-001, quarterly. Ottawa: National Accounts and Environment Division.

Statistics Canada (various issues). Public Sector Finance, Financial Management System, Public Institutions Division, Electronic data.

Statistics Canada (various issues). *Compendium of Public Sector Statistics*. Ottawa: Supply and Services Canada.

Statistics Canada (various issues). *Provincial Economic Accounts, Annual Estimates*. Cat. 13-213XD. Ottawa: National Accounts and Environment Division.